CLIMBING GUIDE
TO THE CUILLIN OF SKYE

CLIMBING GUIDE

TO

THE CUILLIN OF SKYE

EDITED BY

WILLIAM M. MacKENZIE

PUBLISHED BY

THE SCOTTISH MOUNTAINEERING CLUB
SYNOD HALL, CASTLE TERRACE, EDINBURGH
1958

PRINTED IN GREAT BRITAIN BY
ROBERT CUNNINGHAM AND SONS LTD., ALVA

FOREWORD

THE preparation of this Guide has necessarily covered an extended period during which a large number of people rendered service in the field. Particularly I would like to thank D. Stewart, C. M. Dixon and W. D. Brooker for their work in this connection, Donald Mill for certain diagrams, and to R. Jamieson who, at short notice, resketched all the diagrams.

I am also indebted to the former editors of the Guide to the Island of Skye—E. W. Steeple, Guy Barlow, Harry MacRobert and J. H. B. Bell, whose work it has been my privilege to carry on.

WILLIAM M. MACKENZIE
Editor

5

INTRODUCTION

IN the description of the Black Cuillin we begin at the northern end of the range and work our way south describing each mountain and its climbs, also the lateral ridges, as we come to them.

The climbs have been classified for nails unless otherwise stated.

Right and left has been applied when facing the mountain and also when facing a gully, crack or chimney.

The length of many of the climbs is approximate as they are roughly measured; some of the shorter ones have not been measured at all. This also applies to some short gullies. Measuring the latter routes would entail what is considered a great deal of unnecessary and unimportant work.

Knowledge of winter climbing is very scanty but the experience of Club members and others is that fairly easy excursions become major undertakings. The West Ridge of Sgurr nan Gillean is one of them. The Pinnacle Ridge has never been done when plastered with snow and ice. The round of Coire Lagan probably could not be completed in a day. Those climbs should only be attempted by competent parties.

CONTENTS

DIAGRAMS

A GUIDE TO THE CUILLIN

INTRODUCTORY

THE group of the Cuillin lies in Lat. 57°10′ to 57°16′; W. Long. 6°4′ to 6°17′. Ordnance Survey Map, 6-inch scale, "Island of Skye, Inverness-shire" Sheets 38, 39, 44 and 45; 1-inch scale Popular Edition, Nos. 24, 25, 34 and 35; but owing to the small scale, these are not of great practical use. The Scottish Mountaineering Club publish an outline contour map of the Cuillin, scale about 3 inches to a mile, for special use in connection with this Guide.

The Cuillin consists of two groups, the Red and the Black Cuillin, divided from each other by Glen Sligachan. From Sgurr na h-Uamha in the north to Gars-bheinn in the south they form a continuous chain, the highest summits being linked together by high ridges, which, though broken into many bealachs, rarely fall much below 3000 feet. On both sides of the main chain are lateral ridges, between which lie numerous wild corries, including the huge hollow of Coruisk, the bed of which is 200 feet below the level of the sea. Neither in the corries nor on the mountain sides is there much vegetation for the gabbro when disintegrated does not readily form a soil suitable for plants. The summits are of naked rock, blue-black or purple in colour, while the corries contain the debris torn off from the peaks above, and tossed into a state of inconceivable chaos. On account of their chain-like formation, the Cuillin have always lent themselves to the form of climbing known as "ridge-wandering" which can be enjoyed here as nowhere else in Scotland.

The traverse of the main ridge is undoubtedly the
finest expedition in the British Isles, particularly if
Blaven and Clach Glas are included. The total ascent
amounts to over 13,000 feet, and the first complete
traverse was made by I. G. Charleson and W. E. Forde
in June 1939.* Average good weather traverse time is
about 10-13 hours; if Blaven and Clach Glas are included,
5-6 hours extra may be allowed for.

To those climbers whose experience has been confined
to comparatively easy mountains we give this piece of
advice. Do not be over-ambitious; climb with care.
The rock in the Cuillin is not always quite reliable,
although gabbro has often been described as painfully
adhesive and the great slabs can be walked over at quite
astonishing angles.

There are magnetic deflections almost everywhere,
therefore do not rely on the infallibility of a compass; it
is a simple matter to stray on to difficult rocks in mist
or bad weather.

Centres. The two principal centres are Sligachan and
Glen Brittle. The accommodation at Sligachan is
limited to one hotel. Glen Brittle has Mrs MacRae at
the Lodge, Mr Campbell at Cuillin Cottage, Mr
Sutherland, Mrs Macdonald at the Post Office and the
Youth Hostel. There are bus connections from Kyleakin
to Sligachan and Glen Brittle.

* The first complete traverse, including Clach Glas and
Blaven, by a woman, was made in July, 1956.

EASY EXCURSIONS FROM SLIGACHAN AND GLEN BRITTLE

Loch Coruisk. From Sligachan Hotel cross the bridge and follow the rough path up the east side of Glen Sligachan for four miles, then leave the pathway (which continues on to Camasunary) just beyond the Dubh lochs, and breast the shoulder of the Druim Hain ridge. A rough pathway leads to the top of the ridge, but beyond that the path must be left and a way made to the right down to the loch-side. The continuation of the path merely leads to a good view-point. It takes some three hours' steady walking to reach the loch.

The expedition can be extended as follows:

1. A circuit of Loch Coruisk may be made.

2. The east shore of Loch Scavaig may be followed round to Camasunary. This includes the passage of the much-dreaded "bad step", on which there is not the slightest difficulty if crossed at the right place. Most people who get into trouble here attempt to cross too high up, for the step is only about 15 feet above high-water level. The correct way is more easily found in going to Camasunary from Loch Coruisk than in the reverse direction.

3. Should the tourist be more ambitious he may, from the head of Loch Coruisk, continue up the valley and cross the Bealach na Glaic Moire (2510 feet) to Coire na Creiche, returning to Sligachan by the Bealach a' Mhaim.

Short-cuts may be made from Glen Sligachan to the head of Loch Coruisk via the Bloody Stone in Harta Corrie by crossing the Druim nan Ramh ridge at its lowest point, but a stranger is apt to lose time among the huge ice-worn boiler-plate slabs on the Coruisk side of this unless he hits off the right place.

Bruach na Frithe. One of the best view-points within reach of Sligachan is Bruach na Frithe (3143 feet). No rock-climbing is necessary to reach the top. The ascent can be made by the north-west ridge from the Bealach a' Mhaim in two hours, returning by Fionn Choire, or along the easy ridge of Sgurr a' Bhasteir.

Coire na Creiche. One of the favourite excursions from Sligachan is over the Bealach a' Mhaim to Coire na Creiche. The route lies to the left at the Bealach, and is marked by cairns. Instead of merely admiring the picturesque corries, the pedestrian should continue on into the left corrie—Coir' a' Mhadaidh—and climb up scree slopes to the main ridge just north of Bidein. A descent may be made on the far side to Harta Corrie, and Sligachan reached by the Glen.

The Mam (or Meall a' Mhaim, 1335 feet), close to the Bealach a' Mhaim, and only some 200 feet above it, on its north-west side, is a magnificent place for an evening view, when the western sun is painting the rocks of Coire na Creiche.

Sgurr na Banachdich (3167 feet) is one of the easiest of the high Cuillin. By going round Sgurr Thuilm, past Coire a' Ghreadaidh and up Coir' an Eich, it can be done leisurely from Sligachan in four hours, and about three hours back.

Red Hills. The ascent of Glamaig from Sligachan takes about one hour and twenty minutes, and the descent forty minutes.

In a short day one can easily make a circular tour of the near Red Hills, by going over Glamaig, Beinn Dearg Mhor, Beinn Dearg Mheadhonach, and Druim na Ruaige.

Marsco. Follow a route rising gradually along the northern face on to the ridge on the west side of Coire nan Laogh. Descend by that little corrie for a change.

The following Table of Times may be useful to the climber in calculating how much time to allow to get home, from a given point, without any halts:

To Sligachan:		hr.	m.
From Bealach a' Mhaim . . .		1	0
,, head of Coire na Creiche . .		1	30
,, Coire a' Ghreadaidh . . .		2	30
,, Bealach na Glaic Moire . .		2	0
,, Glen Brittle House (over Bealach a' Mhaim)		2	30
,, the march-fence in Glen Sligachan (near Marsco Burn) . . .		0	40
,, Loch an Athain		1	30
,, Druim Hain (by west side of valley)		2	0
,, Loch a' Bhasteir		1	0
,, Loch Scavaig (over Druim Hain)		3	0
,, head of Loch Coruisk (over Druim Hain)		3	10
,, Camasunary Ford (by west side of Loch na Creitheach) easy going		2	30

To Glen Brittle House:		hr.	m.
From Bealach Coire na Banachdich .		1	10
,, Bealach Coire Lagan . . .		1	0
,, top of Sgurr Dearg . . .		1	0
,, Loch Coire Lagan . . .		0	45
,, top of Alasdair Stone Shoot .		1	20
,, top of Sgurr na Banachdich (by Coir' an Eich)		1	10

At Sligachan on wet days the disconsolate climber can fish for sea-trout (in August or September).

He may also scramble about the gorge of the small burn that joins the Sligachan River nearly opposite the hotel. (A deep pool can be "traversed" by a series of tiny ledges, up one side and down the other.)

The Eagle's Nest Crag gives good sport (p. 39). There is also good climbing on the rocky knoll to the east of the Tourist Route to Sgurr nan Gillean, and ¼ mile south-east of the First Pinnacle (p. 33).

Three good climbing excursions from Sligachan may be recommended to strangers with only a few days to spare:

1. *Sgurr nan Gillean*, going up by the Pinnacles and down by the western ridge (p. 34). The best way to the base of the First Pinnacle is via the old keeper's cottage (Cuillin Lodge), cross the Red Burn there by stepping-stones, and make for the left (west) bank of the burn that comes out of the Bhasteir ravine, cross the stream below the ravine, and follow the rounded ridge which leads up to the lowest pinnacle. The streams among the Cuillin often come down in sudden spate, and may become unfordable after a few hours of heavy rain. When the stepping-stones are covered, the Red Burn may be crossed by a foot-bridge lower down.

2. *The round of Coire Lagan*. By motoring to Glen Brittle, one can ascend Sgurr Sgumain, Alasdair, Thearlaich, Mhic Coinnich, and the Inaccessible Pinnacle of Sgurr Dearg, and return to Sligachan at night. From the Inaccessible Pinnacle to Sligachan the best way, if the climber is fairly fresh, is to go over Banachdich and Ghreadaidh, down into Tairneilear and over the Bealach a' Mhaim.

3. *Clach Glas and Blaven*. A traverse of these fine peaks, with or without Garbh-bheinn thrown in, forms an enjoyable expedition of about ten hours, and gives a fair amount of rock-climbing of moderate difficulty (pp. 126-128).

From Glen Brittle the following are good walks for off-days:

1. Along the top of the sea-cliffs between Loch Brittle and the foot of Gars-bheinn, or round the peninsula to Loch Eynort.

2. The gorge and waterfall on the burn called Allt a' Coire a' Ghreadaidh is worth exploring, and gives a sporting bit of chimney work above a pool 10 feet deep.

3. For a wet day, the waterfall (Eas Mor) on the Allt Coire na Banachdich deserves a visit. There are few finer falls in Scotland when in spate. It is best seen from the left bank of the burn.

EASY PASSES ACROSS THE MAIN RIDGE

There are several routes across the main ridge, and the three following may be found useful:

1. *Bealach nan Lice* (2940 feet). From ¾ of a mile on the Sligachan side of the summit of the Bealach a' Mhaim turn up Fionn Choire, cross the pass just under the Tooth of Bhasteir (this point can also be easily reached by the Bhasteir Corrie, but the "going" there, though perhaps more interesting, is somewhat rougher), then descend the steep screes to Lota Corrie, and by keeping the left bank of the stream, which falls into Harta Corrie, the latter can be easily reached.

2. *Bealach na Glaic Moire* (2510 feet). Cross the Bealach a' Mhaim and pass through Coire na Creiche to Coir' a' Mhadaidh, ascend the shoulder of Sgurr an Fheadain, close under the nearest peak of Bidein. Then cross the pass, which lies south-west of all the Bidein peaks. A long scree slope descends to Coruisk. It has two branches near the top. It does not matter which one is taken; but the one to the north is easier to descend, and the one to the south is the better to ascend by. The above route by Coir' a' Mhadaidh is recommended in preference to that by Tairneilear, for more than one person has got into difficulties on the loose scree of the latter route. When coming from Coruisk, however, in clear weather, the Tairneilear route is the natural way, and no difficulty should be found in the descent.

3. *Bealach Coire na Banachdich* (2785 feet). This is the easiest pass from Glen Brittle to Coruisk if the proper route be taken. The chief point to be remembered after

getting to the first steep ascent in Coire na Banachdich is to keep to the right, up a gully leading to the cliffs of Sgurr Dearg till a traverse can be made to the bealach. The descent on the Coruisk side is over screes, then keep to the right or south until some smooth rocks at about 1800 feet are passed.

THE PEAKS AND PASSES
OF THE CUILLIN

Many of the heights of peaks given in the last edition of the 6-inch map of the Ordnance Survey have been found to be incorrect, and in this Guide these heights have been replaced by values obtained from trigonometrical measurements and levelling made by Dr G. Barlow in 1922 (S.M.C.J., vol. xvi). In the more important cases attention is called to the correction by giving the O.S. value in [   ]. The O.S. heights are indicated by an asterisk, with the addition of (T.S.) for trigonometrical stations.

The heights of bealachs and of a few minor peaks are based chiefly on aneroid readings made by members of the S.M.C. Where these values have not been sufficiently checked they are marked "ap."

The Main Group

Sgurr nan Gillean, 3167* (T.S.), lies 3 m. S.S.W. of Sligachan Hotel.

(a) From the summit a branch ridge runs N.N.E., dividing Coire a' Bhasteir on the W. from Glen Sligachan on the E. This is the Pinnacle Ridge. The fourth pinnacle, or Knight's Peak, lying next to Sgurr nan Gillean, is 3000 ap. The third is 2900 ap.; the second, 2700 ap.; and the first, 2500 ap.

(b) From the summit a branch ridge runs S.E., dividing Lota Corrie on the W. from Coire nan Allt Geala on the E. It ends in **Sgurr na h-Uamha,** 2420 ap., pron. *Sgurr na Hoo-a,* which lies 1 m. S. by E. from Sgurr nan Gillean. The lowest point on this ridge is 2050 ap. A small peak lies between

18

this and Sgurr nan Gillean, $\frac{1}{2}$ m. S.E. by S. from the latter, and is called on the 6-inch map **Sgurr Beag,** 2530 ap. This is the ridge by which the tourist makes the ascent. He joins it between the summit and Sgurr Beag at a height of 2360 ap.

From the summit the main ridge runs westward to the Tooth of Sgurr nan Gillean and

Coire a' Bhasteir	BEALACH A' BHASTEIR, 2780 ap. (an easy pass)	Lota Corrie

Am Basteir, 3070, $\frac{1}{2}$ m. W. of Sgurr nan Gillean.

Bhasteir Tooth, 3000, lies immediately under Am Basteir to the W.

(*a*) From 50 yards W. of the Tooth a branch ridge runs N. for $\frac{1}{4}$ m., with a dip at 2865 ap., and ending in **Sgurr a' Bhasteir,** 2950 ap. It separates Fionn Choire from Coire a' Bhasteir.

Fionn Choire	BEALACH NAN LICE, 2940 ap. pron. *Leeka* (an easy pass, see p. 16). This was formerly called BEALCH A' LEITIR.	Lota Corrie

Sgurr a' Fionn Choire, 3065, a small peak immediately W. of the pass.

Fionn Choire	Dip, 2970 ap.	Lota Corrie

Bruach na Frithe, 3143 * (T.S.), pron. *Bruach na Free*, $\frac{3}{4}$ m. W. of Sgurr nan Gillean.

(*a*) From the summit a branch ridge runs N.W. to Sron an Tobar nan Uaislean, 1682,* and Bealach a' Mhaim, 1132.*

From the summit of Bruach na Frithe the main ridge turns to the S., running without any well-marked break to

Coir' a' Mhadaidh	Dip, 2760 ap.	Lota Corrie

Sgurr na Bhairnich, 2830 ap., lies ½ m. S. of the summit of Bruach na Frithe.

Coir' a' Mhadaidh | Dip, 2520 ap. This deeply cut cleft is one of the lowest points of the main ridge. Descent into Coir' a' Mhadaidh by a stone shoot. From the gully on the E. side it is possible to reach Lota Corrie by short rock wall just above where the gully takes a great plunge down the lower precipices. | Harta Corrie

An Caisteal, 2730 ap.

Coir' a' Mhadaidh BEALACH, 2510 (an easy pass). Harta Corrie

North Peak, Bidein Druim nan Ramh, 2790, pron. *Bidyin Drim na Raav*, lies ¾ m. S.S.W. of Bruach na Frithe.

Coir' a' Mhadaidh   Gap, 2700 ap.   Harta Corrie

Central (or South-East) Peak, Bidein Druim nan Ramh, 2850, lies about 70 yards S.S.W. of the North Peak.

  (*a*) From the Central Peak a branch ridge called **Druim nan Ramh** runs S.E. for 2½ m., dividing Harta Corrie from Coruisk. Before terminating this ridge sends off an eastward extension to the parallel ridge of **Druim Hain,** and **Sgurr Hain,** and thence S.W. to the isolated **Sgurr na Stri,** 1623 * overlooking Loch Scavaig.

Coir' a' Mhadaidh | Gap, with natural bridge, 2710 ap. (an easy scree gully for descent into Coir' a' Mhadaidh). | Glaic Moire and Coruisk

West Peak, Bidein Druim nan Ramh, 2780, lies about 60 yards W. by N. of the Central Peak.

  (*a*) From the West Peak a branch ridge runs for ½ m. N.W. towards Coire na Creiche and ends with **Sgurr an Fheadain,** 2215 ap., pron. *Sgurr an*

Aityan. This ridge divides Coir' a' Mhadaidh on the N.E. from Tairneilear on the S.W.

From the West Peak the main ridge runs nearly W. to

Tairneilear	BEALACH NA GLAIC MOIRE, 2510 ap. (see p. 16).	Glaic Moire and Coruisk

North-East Peak, Sgurr a' Mhadaidh, 2935, pron. *Sgurr a Vatee,* 1 m. S.W. from Bruach na Frithe.

Tairneilear	Dip, 2852	Coire an Uaigneis and Coruisk

Second Peak, Sgurr a' Mhadaidh, 2907.

Tairneilear	Dip, 2851	Coire an Uaigneis

Third Peak, Sgurr a' Mhadaidh, 2925.

Tairneilear	Dip, 2810 (Descent into Coire an Uaigneis by an easy rake.)	Coire an Uaigneis

The ridge is here complicated by sheets of gabbro cutting it obliquely. After passing a small pinnacle and a gap 20 ft. deep the direction of the ridge turns abruptly S. to

South-West Peak, Sgurr a' Mhadaidh, 3010. This peak has a summit ridge running S. from a point 2970, near the above-mentioned pinnacle, to the highest point 3010 (cairn), without dipping more than 5 ft. The top is a narrow crest-line connecting the cairned point with another point of equal height 30 ft. beyond.

(*a*) From the northern end of the summit ridge, the point 2970 (wrongly indicated as the summit and marked 3014 on the O.S. map), a shattered ridge dividing Tairneilear from Coire na Dorus runs W.N.W. to **Sgurr Thuilm,** 2885 * (T.S.), pron. *Hulim,* with a bealach at 2450 ap.

The main ridge continues S. to

AN DORUS, 2760. (This is marked An Dorus on the O.S. map.) The descent into Coire na Dorus is easy. On the Coruisk side there is a narrow gully with several small pitches.

Coire na Dorus the N.E. branch of Coire a' Ghreadaidh

Coire an Uaigneis

From this pass the ridge rising to Sgurr a' Ghreadaidh is interrupted by a narrow gap now known as EAG DUBH, 2890. An easy scree gully leads into Coire na Dorus, but the only approach on the Coruisk side is by a difficult gully.

North Top, Sgurr a' Ghreadaidh, 3190 [3197 *], pron. *Sgurr Greeta*, lies ½ m. S. of the S.W. peak of Sgurr a' Mhadaidh. Sgurr a' Ghreadaidh has a long narrow crestline with two summits, besides a wart-like prominence just N. of the chief summit.

(*a*) In a direction N.W. from this prominence, but starting about 200 ft. down on the western face, a spur runs off with successive points at about 2870 and 2770. These have been named **Sgurr Eadar da Choire.**

Dip between the tops, 3110.

South Top, Sgurr a' Ghreadaidh, 3180.

(*a*) From the summit of the south top a short branch ridge runs E.S.E., dividing Coire an Uaigneis from Coireachan Ruadha.

Dip, 2780.

Coire a' Ghreadaidh, south branch

Not a pass, but descent into Coire a' Ghreadaidh can be made without much difficulty.

Coireachan Ruadha and Coruisk

Three small teeth, 2950.

Dip, 2925.

Sgurr Thormaid, 3040, lies scarcely ½ m. S.W. of Sgurr a' Ghreadaidh. It was formerly called the North Top of Banachdich.

    (a) From here a short spur runs into Coire a' Ghreadaidh.

Coire a' Ghreadaidh, south branch | BEALACH, 2920. Descent into Coire a' Ghreadaidh, first a short rough scramble, then easy, turning to right round "short spur". Descent into Coireachan Ruadha presents no difficulty except from unstable screes. | Coireachan Ruadha

North Top (highest), Sgurr na Banachdich, 3167 * (T.S.).

    (a) From the summit a long branch ridge, **Sgurr nan Gobhar,** runs off to W., terminating at a cairn 2047 * (T.S.). From this ridge, at about 2700, the shorter spur of **An Diallaid** runs off to N.W., with a dip 2365 and summit 2375. There is an easy descent by way of Coir' an Eich lying between Sgurr nan Gobhar and An Diallaid.

Coire na Banachdich   Dip, 3010 ap.   Coireachan Ruadha

Second Top, Sgurr na Banachdich, 3090 ap.

Coire na Banachdich   Dip, 2970 ap.   Coireachan Ruadha

Third Top, Sgurr na Banachdich, 3010 ap.

Coire na Banachdich   Dip, 2830 ap. (alternative pass).   Coireachan Ruadha

Southern End of Banachdich Range, 2880 ap.

    (a) From here a spur, **Sron Bhuidhe,** about 2650, runs off to E.N.E., dividing Coireachan Ruadha into two small corries.

BEALACH COIRE NA BAN-
ACHDICH, 2785 ap. This is
probably the easiest pass
between Glen Brittle and
Coruisk. See p. 16.

Coire na
Banachdich

Coireachan
Ruadha

Gap just before precipice of Dearg, 2910 ap.

Sgurr Dearg, 3206 [O.S. 3234 * T.S.], pron. *Sgurr
Jerrack* (named "Inaccessible Peak", 3212, on the
Admiralty Chart), lies ½ m. S.S.E. of Sgurr na Banach-
dich.

(a) From the cairn of Sgurr Dearg a ridge dividing
Coire na Banachdich from Coire Lagan runs S.
to a slight dip, then W. to a marked summit 3042,*
and terminates at the cairn of **Sron Dearg,** 2012.*
From a point about 2535 on this ridge a short spur
called the Window Tower Buttress runs off N.W.,
with tower at 2190.

Dip, 3175.

Inaccessible Pinnacle, 3226 [O.S. 3254 *], lies 100
feet S.S.E. of the cairn.

[*N.B.* This part of the ridge is not clearly shown on
the O.S. map. The O.S. heights for Sgurr Dearg and for
the Pinnacle are nearly 28 feet too great relatively to the
other trigonometrical stations.]

The main ridge continues in a general S.E. direction to
Dip, 3090.

An Stac, 3125 = the stack. An easy descent from Sgurr
Dearg to Coire Lagan can be made over screes, skirting
W. base of Inaccessible Pinnacle and An Stac, and
bearing to left till near the bealach. The scree leading
more directly towards the corrie over a precipice should
be avoided.

BEALACH COIRE LAGAN, 2655. Descent into Coireachan Ruadha troublesome for the first 300 or 400 feet, having rotten rock at top and smooth slabs below; the latter may be avoided by keeping away to the left.

Coire Lagan

Coireachan Ruadha and Coruisk

The gap, 2595, about 120 yards S.E. of bealach is the lowest point, but is not a pass.

Sgurr Mhic Coinnich, 3107 * lies ½ m. S.E. of Sgurr Dearg.

BEALACH MHIC COINNICH, 2935 ap. Descent into Coire Lagan—first a short rock scramble, then a scree gully joining the Alasdair Stone Shoot at about 2500. Descent on other side into Coireachan Ruadha, or on to col of Sgurr Coire an Lochain, presents no difficulty.

Coire Lagan

Coireachan Ruadha

Sgurr Thearlaich, 3201. This used to be called the N.E. Peak of Alasdair.

(a) From the northern end of Sgurr Thearlaich a ridge, at first ill defined, runs N.E. for ½ m., separating Coireachan Ruadha from Coir' an Lochain. After a dip at 2440 the ridge rises to **Sgurr Coire an Lochain,** with highest point 2480, which is divided by a deep gap, 2330, from the north top, 2390.

Leaving the main ridge at Sgurr Thearlaich to traverse the important ridge to the S.W., there is from the summit a steep descent to

Coire Lagan

Dip, 3130. Head of "Great Stone Shoot" from Coire Lagan. A severe rock-climb on the Ghrunnda side.

Coir' a' Ghrunnda

Sgurr Alasdair, 3251 [*N.B.* The O.S. height, 3309, is incorrect.] lies close to and W. of Sgurr Thearlaich. It is the highest peak in Skye.

From the summit a ridge runs S.W. to

Dip, 3020.

Coire Lagan   Descent over screes on either   Coir' a' Ghrunnda
side.

Sgurr Sgumain, 3104 * (T.S.), lies 200 yards S.W. of Sgurr Alasdair. From near the summit subsidiary ridges run W. and N.W. into Coire Lagan. To the S.S.W. the principal ridge continues to

BEALACH COIR' A' GHRUNNDA,

Coire Lagan   2735.   Coir' a' Ghrunnda
(A useful pass).

Beyond this the ridge broadens out into the sloping stony plateau of **Sron na Ciche,** named from the remarkable pinnacle Cioch a' Sgumain on its Coire Lagan face.

Returning to Sgurr Thearlaich the main ridge runs S.E. to

THEARLAICH—DUBH GAP,

Coir' a' Ghrunnda   2950 ap. Descent of gully to Coir' a' Ghrunnda of moderate difficulty. Other side of Gap apparently hopeless.   Coir' an Lochain

The S.E. wall of the Gap forms a pinnacle, 2980 ap., from which the ridge drops to

Coir' a' Ghrunnda   BEALACH COIR' AN LOCHAIN, 2820 ap. Descent into Coir' a' Ghrunnda easy. If continuing down the corrie, leave the burn where it turns to left after first steep descent, and passing just below a rough bit of scree, keep up on W. side of Corrie, thus avoiding glaciated slabs. Descent into Coir' an   Coir' an Lochain

Coir' a' Ghrunnda Lochain rough. There is an easy way to Coruisk from Coir' an Lochain. At the mouth of the corrie, on the right, a cairn marks the top of this way. One may walk straight down a ledge which runs eastwards to Coir' a' Chaoruinn, emerging into this through a small natural arch at about 1200 feet altitude. *Coir' an Lochain*

Sgurr Dubh na Da Bheinn, 3069,* pron. *Sgurr Doo na Da Ven*, lies nearly ½ m. E.S.E. of Sgurr Alasdair.

From this peak a long ridge runs E. to

An Garbh-choire	Dip, 2900 ap.	Coir' an Lochain

Sgurr Dubh Mor, 3089,* pron. *Sgurr Doo Mor*, lies ¼ m. E. of Sgurr Dubh na Da Bheinn. (From the summit a branch ridge runs to the N., separating Coir' an Lochain from Coir' a' Chaoruinn.)

An Garbh-choire	Dip, 2280 ap.	Coir' a' Chaoruinn

On the E. side of this dip there is a very steep ascent to **Sgurr Dubh Beag,** 2420 ap., lies ½ m. E. of Sgurr Dubh Mor.

From the summit the ridge continues eastwards for 1 m. in an unbroken line of slabs to the shore of Loch Coruisk.

Returning to the main ridge, from Sgurr Dubh na Da Bheinn it runs S. to

Coir' a' Ghrunnda	Dip, 2620 ap.	An Garbh-choire

Caisteal a' Gharbh-choire, 2740 ap., stands at the head of An Garbh-choire.

Coir' a' Ghrunnda BEALACH A' GHARBH-CHOIRE, 2620 ap. (an easy pass). The direct way down the bottom of An Garbh-choire is made difficult by a chaos of huge blocks of rock; an easier route can be found by keeping to the flank of Sgurr Dubh. *An Garbh-choire*

Sgurr nan Eag, 3037 * (T.S.), lies ½ m. S. of Sgurr Dubh na Da Bheinn. It has a nearly level summit ridge running S.E. for 300 or 400 yards. A broad sloping shoulder extends to the S.W., separating Coir' a' Ghrunnda from Coire nan Laogh.

Coire nan Laogh | BEALACH, 2550. To reach Coire nan Laogh easily, either ascend to the shoulder of Sgurr nan Eag or keep up on the slope of Sgurr a' Choire Bhig at first. Descent into An Garbh-choire, bearing to left for the first 100 feet. | An Garbh-choire

Sgurr a' Choire Bhig, 2880 ap., pron. *Sgurr a Corrie Vick,* lies over ½ m. E.S.E. of Sgurr nan Eag.

(*a*) From the summit a branch ridge runs off N.E., dividing An Garbh-choire from Coire Beag.

Coire nan Laogh | Dip, 2760 ap. (a possible pass). Descent into Coire nan Laogh, at first keep well up on slopes of Garsbheinn. Descent into Coire Beag difficult at first, keeping close under Sgurr a' Choire Bhig; then bearing well to right to avoid slabs. | Coire Beag

Gars-bheinn, 2934 * (T.S.), pron. *Garsven* (named Gairs-bheinn, 2902, on the Admiralty Chart), lies 1 m. S.E. of Sgurr nan Eag.

(*a*) From a point a little S. of the summit a branch ridge runs off N.E., dividing Coire Beag from Coir' a' Chruidh (corrie of the cattle), and terminating in a pinnacled crag at about 2125.

The main ridge from Gars-bheinn continues in the S.E. direction to

Prominent point on ridge, 2665 ap. A little beyond this another branch ridge runs off N.E. into Coir' a' Chruidh, terminating at about 1850.

Ridge continues E.S.E., with a prominent point at 2485 and another at the termination 2275.

The Red Hills

Glamaig, 2537,* lies 2 m. E. of Sligachan. The highest top is named Sgurr Mhairi. The E. summit is called An Coileach.

Bealach na Sgairde, 1419

Beinn Dearg Mhor, 2389,* lies 1 m. S. of Glamaig.

Bealach Mosgaraidh, 1663

Beinn Dearg Mheadhonach, 2094,* lies 2 m. S. of Glamaig.

Ciche na Beinne Deirge, 1661,* lies ½ m. S. of Beinn Dearg Mheadhonach.

Coire Dubh Measarroch
Mam
a' Phobuill, 952.
Coire nan Bruadaran

Marsco, 2414,* lies 3 m. S. of Glamaig.

Am Fraoch-choire   Bealach, 1079.   Coire nan Bruadaran

The Blaven Group

Garbh-bheinn, 2649,* 'pron. Garaven', lies 1 m. N. of Blaven.

From here a branch ridge runs N.E. to

Bealach na Beiste, an easy pass.

Belig, 2250 ap., 2 m. N.E. of Blaven.

Bealach

Glas-bheinn Mhor, 1852,* lies 1½ m. N.N.E. of Belig. The main ridge from Garbh-bheinn runs S.E. to

Bealach, 2086,* an easy pass.

Sgurr nan Each, W. Top, 2360,* lies 1 m. N.E. of Blaven. The E. Top, 2400,* is about ¼ m. E. of W. Top. Dip, 2060 ap.

Clach Glas, 2590, lies ⅓ m. N.E. of Blaven. The O.S. map names this "Glac Glas", evidently a misprint.

BEALACH, 2310, an easy pass.

Blaven, N. Top, 3042 * (T.S.), lies 2 m. N.N.E. of
Camasunary.

Dip, 2980 ap.

Blaven, S. Top, 3031.*

From the N. and S. tops short ridges run out E. and
S.E. respectively, enclosing Coire Uaigneis.

From the S. top the main ridge continues S.S.W. for
1 m. to its termination.

BROADFORD GROUP OF RED HILLS

Beinn na Caillich, 2403,* lies 2½ m. W. of Broadford.

Beinn Dearg Mhor, 2323, lies 1 m. W.S.W. of Beinn
na Caillich.

Beinn Dearg Bheag, 1750 cont., lies 1 m. S.W. of Beinn
na Caillich.

PEAKS ARRANGED IN ORDER OF ALTITUDE

3251	Sgurr Alasdair	3010	Sgurr a' Mhadaidh
3226	Inaccessible Pinnacle		S.W. Peak
3206	Sgurr Dearg	3000	Bhasteir Tooth
3201	Sgurr Thearlaich	2934*	Gars-bheinn
3190	Sgurr a' Ghreadaidh	2885*	Sgurr Thuilm
3167*	Sgurr nan Gillean	2880	Sgurr a' Choire Bhig
3167*	Sgurr na Banachdich	2850	Bidein Druim nan Ramh, Central Peak
3143*	Bruach na Frithe		
3125	An Stac		
3107*	Sgurr Mhic Coinnich	2830	Sgurr na Bhairnich
3104*	Sgurr Sgumain	2730	An Caisteal
3089*	Sgurr Dubh Mor	2649*	Garbh-bheinn
3070	Am Basteir	2590	Clach Glas
3069*	Sgurr Dubh na Da Bheinn	2537*	Glamaig
		2530	Sgurr Beag

3065	Sgurr a' Fionn Choire	2480	Sgurr Coire an Lochain
3042*	Blaven		
3040	Sgurr Thormaid	2420	Sgurr Dubh Beag
3037*	Sgurr nan Eag	2420	Sgurr na h-Uamha
		2414*	Marsco
		2403*	Beinn na Caillich

ROUTES AND ROCK CLIMBS ON THE CUILLIN

SGURR NAN GILLEAN (3617 feet)

Sgurr nan Gillean has three well-defined ridges running respectively south-east, north and west.

THE "TOURIST ROUTE" joins the south-east ridge near the col between "Sgurr Beag" and the summit. It bears south over the moor, after crossing the Red Burn by stepping stones; or a footbridge further down can be used. After crossing a low ridge the loch in Coire Riabhach is passed a quarter mile off on the left. The Coirenan allt Geala is reached by climbing an easy stone shoot, and the south-east ridge is ultimately gained by mounting a long scree slope. Then turning to the right, the ridge can be followed to the summit. The only place where hands need be used is on the last 100 feet but it is not really difficult.

The prominent rock face on the left of the "Tourist Route" as seen from Sligachan gives a climb partly in the left hand of two gullies and partly by the face.

PINNACLE RIDGE (NORTH RIDGE)   Difficult

This is the nearest expedition to Sligachan and can, coupled with the descent of the Western Ridge, be accomplished in five to six hours. From Sligachan the ridge is seen end-on and its peaks cannot be distinguished easily one from the other. There are four pinnacles—1, 2, 3, 4, going upwards and the fourth is sometimes called "Knight's Peak".

The N.W. ridge of the First Pinnacle is the usual

c

approach and is easy. From the First to the Second and Third Pinnacles is only a walk along the ridge, the climbing beginning at the foot of the Third Pinnacle. The route is too well marked for further description, involving about 600 feet of ascent and 200 feet descent.

WEST RIDGE   MODERATE

From the top of Sgurr nan Gillean the West Ridge extends to Bealach a' Bhasteir. It is noted for its fine gendarme. There is an abrupt drop just beyond the gendarme (i.e. descending) which can be turned on the north side by a 40-foot chimney.

SLIGACHAN FACE OF FIRST PINNACLE
(250/300 feet)

Several climbs have been recorded on this face above Coire Riabbach. It is divided into two sections—a lower and an upper—by a broad scree-covered shelf.

NAISMITH'S ROUTE   DIFFICULT

The lower tier—steep rocks 70 yards to left of gully prominent from Sligachan as a well marked gash (Black Chimney). The upper tier—by a 40-foot chimney and a steep rock wall above it.

First ascent by W. W. Naismith and party in 1896.

BLACK CHIMNEY   SEVERE

Steep pitch of 50 feet to a chockstone, pass to the left. An overhanging cave, above this a vertical 30 foot crack (crux).

First ascent by James Maclay and party in 1898.

SLIGACHAN GULLY   DIFFICULT

Nearly straight above the Black Chimney. Straight-forward gully. Feature—boulder pitches.

Alternative to part of gully—to the left by way of two "Parallel Chimneys".

First ascent by A. P. Abraham and H. Harland, *circa* 1907.

SLIGACHAN BUTTRESS   DIFFICULT

To the left of Sligachan Gully and Parallel Chimneys by a few yards. Steep rocks to the top of the buttress.

First ascent by J. M. A. Thomson and party in September 1911.

PINNACLES FROM BHASTEIR COIRE

The face of the First Pinnacle is too broken up to offer definite climbs and the gully between the First and Second Pinnacles is easy.

SECOND PINNACLE (FACE CLIMB)
300 feet   DIFFICULT

Easy in the lower part. Above last terrace, an open chimney for 30 feet. Then a 12-foot traverse to right across slab, traverse back above slab. A difficult upward move then 60 feet to the right below overhang and finally up a steep edge to the summit.

First ascent by J. M. A. Thomson and party in September 1911.

SECOND/THIRD GULLY   DIFFICULT

The only difficulty is getting past a large cave—back and foot.

First ascent by Dr Collier and party in 1896.

THIRD PINNACLE (FACE CLIMBS)
SLINGSBY's ROUTE   400 feet   SEVERE

There is no great difficulty from the foot of the
pinnacle to a ledge on a level with top of first big pitch
in Second/Third Gully (cairn left). In the next 100 feet
are concentrated the chief difficulties. Steep rocks with
small holds lead to the foot of a sharply inclined slab.
Awkward start to slab but once a deep crack on right is
reached it is easy to gain a second broad ledge below a
cave. The exit from the cave is on the left side.

First ascent by W. C. Slingsby and party in 1890.

LÜSCHER's No. 1   400 feet   VERY DIFFICULT

To the right of Slingsby's Route. By a chimney which
crosses the ledge running beneath the steep slab, climb
direct from the scree. Above the ledge three pitches—
the third is difficult. From a ledge continue up rocks
on right to a ridge which falls steeply to Third/Fourth
Gully.

First ascent by Dr Lüscher in August 1920.

LÜSCHER's No. 2   300 feet   DIFFICULT

The second climb starts from the gully at a deep black
crack followed for 15 feet, cross slab on left (small holds).
Then straight up to the ridge on the previous route.

First ascent by Dr Lüscher in August 1920.

THIRD/FOURTH GULLY
300 feet   VERY DIFFICULT

The climbing is practically confined to 100 feet. The
first 70 feet consists of two slimy chimneys then a large
cave. The next pitch is the most difficult one, and on
this the rock is not sound. A short chimney finishes the
climb.

First ascent by R. Lamb and party in 1905.

FOURTH PINNACLE (KNIGHT'S PEAK)
(Face Climbs)

WEST FACE (Ordinary Route)   500 feet   MODERATE

From the vicinity of the subsidiary gully on the Sgurr nan Gillean side of the Pinnacle by numerous routes from this point.

NORTH FACE   500 feet   DIFFICULT

From below the difficult pitch in Third/Fourth Gully along a narrow ledge and then straight up.

First ascent by W. W. King and party in 1898.

Also by first obvious chimney in right-hand side of Third/Fourth Gully. From a shallow cave at its foot, climb the chimney for a short distance, break out on the left and ascend series of fine slabs to the summit.

First ascent by G. D. Abraham, H. Harland and G. Summers in June 1920.

DIRECT FROM THE COIRE   200 feet   SEVERE

At about the middle of the base of the Fourth Pinnacle there is a cave, well known as a shelter. A cairn a few yards to the right of this marks the start of the climb.

Easy climbing leads to a stance at the bottom of a conspicuous groove which slants upwards to the right (20 feet). The groove is followed (30 feet). An upward very difficult traverse to the right over the skyline to a good stance and belay (40 feet).

Twenty feet of difficult climbing leads to a crack. This is followed for about 20 feet without great difficulty, but the exit to the rocks above is on awkwardly placed sloping holds. Eventually a stance is reached immediately under a large overhang, on a 2-inch ledge. Here the climber can rest but there is no belay, and he must with great difficulty traverse about 15 feet to the right, and go up about 5 feet over a nose on small sloping holds to a platform with a good belay. The climber is now on a terrace below the long terrace on the ordinary Fourth Pinnacle face climb, and can, if he wishes, traverse off to the right. On the first ascent a fifth pitch was made by continuing up a steep slab of magnificent rock a few yards above and to the right of the finish of the last pitch. This slab (cairned above and below) leads to a point about midway on the long traverse of the ordinary route, and is severe (95 feet).

First ascent by F. W. Giveen, C. H. Cooper and D. R. Orr on 24th June 1927.

BHASTEIR FACE OF SGURR NAN GILLEAN

FORKED CHIMNEY 200/250 feet VERY DIFFICULT

50 feet to the right of Fourth/Fifth Gully. It is deeply cut, almost vertical, and divides into two about 100 feet above the scree. Keep to the left branch. There is an overhang passed by backing. The right branch also gives a climb.

First ascent by W. W. Naismith and party in 1898.

MACLAREN'S CHIMNEY 150 feet VERY DIFFICULT

To the left of Forked Chimney and near Fourth/Fifth Gully.

First ascent by MacLaren and Shadbolt in September 1911.

FLUTINGS CLIMB   300 feet   DIFFICULT

To the right of Forked Chimney are three shallow gullies; take the one furthest to the right. It is reached by a face climb of about 100 feet.

First ascent by R. Lamb and E. E. Roberts in 1919.

DEEP CHIMNEY   200 feet   DIFFICULT

The chimney starts at the upper left hand corner of the scree shelf on the right of the buttress. Loose scree in the lower part. A feature of this climb is a large jammed block near the top.

First ascent by an S.M.C. party in 1898.

DOCTOR'S GULLIES (Left and Right)   MODERATE

These are parallel to one another, and both start a few feet to the right of the Deep Chimney.

NICOLSON'S CHIMNEY   MODERATELY DIFFICULT

Runs up obliquely to right from near the Doctor's Gullies and strikes the western Ridge of Sgurr nan Gillean just above the "Tooth". It is not an easy route off the Western Ridge.

TOOTH CHIMNEY   100 feet   DIFFICULT

Round a corner from Nicolson's Chimney. Follow left hand side of chimney. Back up round a chock stone and finish on the little col on the Gillean side of the Tooth.

First ascent by W. M. MacKenzie in June 1956.

THE EAGLE'S NEST CRAG

Has a prominent chimney which gives good sport on an off day at Sligachan. The buttress immediately to the left of this chimney was climbed in 1918 by R. W. Lamb and M. G. Bradley, starting up slabs and heather to a conspicuous ledge. A steep 70-foot slab was then climbed to a heather shelf, from which a higher ledge led to the top. This route gives a climb of very difficult standard.

There are other short climbs in chimneys and faces.

SGURR NA H-UAMHA (2420 feet)

This is a beautiful shaped peak, situated about a mile south of Sgurr nan Gillean, and forms the true northern termination of the main Cuillin Ridge.

Its first recorded ascent was made by Charles Pilkington's party in 1896.

SOUTH BUTTRESS

A climb of moderate difficulty can be made on this buttress.

From Harta Corrie—go half mile beyond the Bloody Stone, keep to the left of a gully and follow buttress to the summit. The climbing is over gabbro slabs. There are other routes of a similar standard, nowhere really difficult.

SOUTH-WEST FACE

MURRAY'S CLIMB   1000 feet   DIFFICULT

The south-west buttress springs steeply from the upper part of Harta Corrie. The height from corrie to cairn is probably 1000 feet.

The lower section of the rock-buttress takes the shape of a 350-foot hump, and there is a cairn at the centre of its base line, where one can see into Lota Corrie on the left and Harta Corrie on the right. The climbing of the hump is steep and often exposed, but with adequate holds, and gives five pitches, totalling 320 feet (longest run-out 80 feet). The angle of the buttress then eases off for 150 feet before steepening in overhangs these are turned by a difficult steep slab on the right. One hundred feet of scrambling on fine gabbro slabs leads to the cairn.

First ascent by W. H. Murray and J. K. W. Dunn on 26th June 1937.

SMITH'S CLIMB   1000 feet   SEVERE

The line, chosen to obtain the maximum of continuous climbing, lies south of Murray's route and is roughly in direction of summit from lowest point of Druim nan Ramh ridge. The cliff is arranged in three distinct tiers. The lowest is very broken, the middle is the main face and the upmost the summit rocks. Go up a groove on to very steep slabs for nearly 200 feet, to line of vertical rocks. From below this use a diagonal traverse left to the first steep, smooth groove. The wall is severe. The main face is straight ahead. Climb up until left traverse feasible along a line of trap, then up into a deep, square-cut groove, visible on skyline from bottom of this section. Follow this for 200 feet to summit ridge. This gives 400 feet of difficult rock. Easier scrambling of about 300 feet gains the summit.

First ascent by C. M. G. Smith and R. C. Putman in June 1949.

AM BASTEIR (3070 feet)

TRAVERSE: From Bealach a' Bhasteir to the top of "The Executioner" is an easy scramble along a narrow ridge. From there to the top of the Bhasteir Tooth descend about 80 feet, first down an easy pitch and then a short overhang. There are two ways of passing this difficulty. One route is close to the precipice on the right (north) and the other is a few yards down the Lota Corrie side. It is better for the last man to come down on a doubled rope. There is a third drop which can be turned by a traverse on the Lota Corrie side.

AM BASTEIR CHIMNEY   230 feet   VERY DIFFICULT

This chimney can be divided into three sections. The first part is straightforward, the second part of 70 feet is

the hardest providing back and knee work. The upper
section of 90 feet is fine climbing on excellent holds.

First ascent by J. Martin and R. Mackenzie, who
omitted the middle section, in June 1909. The middle
section was climbed in the same year by K. P. Scoones.

NORTH FACE   DIFFICULT

Climb the first part of the chimney route then traverse
right and upwards across the face coming out, finally,
close to the summit.

BHASTEIR TOOTH (3000 feet)

ORDINARY ROUTE   400 feet   MODERATE

From Lota Corrie, by what can be termed the south-
west ridge. Interesting climbing over slabs and short
chimneys, this is the easiest way to the summit.

First ascent by J. N. Collie in 1889.

The top can be reached from Bealach nan Lice without
the descent into Lota Corrie.

NAISMITH'S   ROUTE   (SOUTH-WEST   FACE
CLIMB)   DIFFICULT

Up easy rocks to the boulder ledge; from the left of
this ledge a short face climb of 15 feet leads to an easy
chimney. Climb this for 20 feet, then follow slanting
crack to the right. Alternatively the climb can be
finished straight up the continuation of the chimney.

First ascent by Naismith and A. M. MacKay in 1898.

NAISMITH'S ROUTE—VARIATION   DIFFICULT

The start is beside a small cave some way below the
col and the first pitch is a 50-foot chimney. There are
three more pitches working upwards to the left, the last

of which is a delicate traversing movement reaching the original route just below the boulder ledge.

First ascent by J. K. W. Dunn and J. G. Wilson in August 1934.

NORTH CHIMNEY (SHADBOLT'S CLIMB)
Difficult

The start is made from the foot of King's Cave up sloping ledges to the foot of the chimney. The first pitch in this is a small cave. There are no great difficulties. Then an easy 40-foot pitch of back and knee to an opening in the roof. This leads to a tunnel going outward for 20 feet doubling back to a small opening (the finish).

First ascent by Shadbolt and MacLaren in 1906.

NORTH CHIMNEY—Variation   Very Difficult

Instead of going into the cave, back up outside to the roof and then outwards horizontally under it and round the end. When the walls get unpleasantly far apart, a large slab of rock which blocks the chimney affords relief by a crack between itself and the east wall. A chockstone can be used here to thread the rope. Constrictive climbing leads to the jumbled blocks at the top of the chimney. Then easy climbing leads finally to two huge blocks, useful as a belay. 100 feet of rope is desirable for two climbers.

First ascent by K. Tarbuck and G. Collin on 3rd June 1932.

KING'S CAVE ROUTE

This route was completely blocked by a collapse of the final tunnel-like chimney in 1924.

SGURR A' FIONN CHOIRE (3065 feet)

Sgurr a' Fionn Choire is the prominent boss of rock between the Bhasteir Tooth and Bruach na Frithe, cleft by a gash at the top. This gash continues in the form of a chimney some distance down the Lota Corrie face.

There is a short climb of moderate difficulty from Lota Corrie. The salient feature is a prominent nose. Ascend the nose on its east side, turn below the overhang and finally the precipitous west side by a steep corner. The rest is easy.

On the wall facing Am Basteir by a steep chimney, traverse a 30° slab to a steep corner on right which leads to a gash near the summit. Moderate.

There is a fine spring, marked by bright green moss, 200 feet below the col between this peak and the Tooth, on the Fionn Choire side.

BRUACH NA FRITHE (3143 feet)

Probably the best viewpoint on the range and is easily ascended by tourists. From Fionn Choire the summit can be reached by a steep scree slope.

NORTH CHIMNEY   DIFFICULT

On the north face by the largest chimney, the upper part of which is difficult consisting of a chockstone not easy to pass.

First ascent by W. W. King and party in 1908.

SGURR NA BHAIRNICH (2830 feet) **and** AN CAISTEAL (2730 feet)

These are the two rocky protuberances with a gash between them, which rise from the main Cuillin Ridge running south from Bruach na Frithe.

There is no difficulty in following the Ridge at this part with the exception of a short stretch of rock on the north end of An Caisteal.

There is not much climbing to be had on the Coire na Creiche side of An Caisteal but the Harta Corrie face is long and steep, and although slabby, some good climbing can be had here. This face is split into three buttresses by two large gullies.

AN CAISTEAL

NORTH BUTTRESS   1000 feet   DIFFICULT

The start is made up the left hand edge of a steep wall and a return made to the centre of the buttress. There follows a long stretch of slabs, gradually getting steeper to a terrace. There is a wall or tower ahead, which is climbed up the front, moving from left to right and then back. The continuation to a final tower is easier. This can be climbed either by a chimney in the centre, or a gully on the left, to a small cairn at its top. From there the top of An Caisteal is easily reached.

First ascent by E. A. Wrangham on 10th May 1953.

CENTRAL BUTTRESS

ARCHER THOMSON'S ROUTE   1200 feet   DIFFICULT

To the left of the North Central Gully. A straight-forward climb, very interesting, no particular features.

First ascent by J. M. A. Thomson and H. O. Jones in 1911.

RAEBURN'S ROUTE   1200 feet   DIFFICULT

To the right of the South/Central Gully. The climb is at first easy, then the rocks become steep and slabby; an overhang is avoided on the left bringing the climb above the gully. A fine chimney leads out above the

overhang by easier rocks. The final wall two-thirds up
the buttress is cleft by several chimneys.

First ascent by H. Raeburn and party in April 1905.

SOUTH BUTTRESS   1000 feet   DIFFICULT

Start by the lowest part of the South/Central Gully,
make a downward traverse to the left by way of a square
platform. Mount the face by steep slabs (route can be
varied) then an easier section of 200 feet whereupon the
buttress narrows to an edge with a precipice on left and
the gully on right.

First ascent by L. G. Shadbolt and A. C. MacLaren
in 1911.

A very difficult start to this climb was made by E. L.
Wigham and C. E. W. Johnson on 30th May 1946.

Climb direct from the bottom of the gully to the platform, ascend a short vertical wall on left of gully where
a large rock splinter projects from the wall. This avoids
an uninteresting and unpleasant detour.

There is no record of the North/Central and South/
Central Gullies having been climbed.

BIDEIN DRUIM NAN RAMH (2850 feet)

The three peaks form a triangle and they are all part
of the main ridge, which bends sharply at the central
(highest) peak and alters its direction from south to west.
The going on the ridge at this point is not easy and from
north to south on the north side of the central peak there
is an overhang. This can be avoided by a traverse on
the west side, but better still take a short vertical pitch
on the left side of the gap, with a sloping slab above it
and regain the crest of the ridge above the overhang.

Bidein can be approached from the north-west by the

ridge of Sgurr an Fheadain, or the south-east by Druim nan Ramh. The latter ridge gives a good scramble of moderate difficulty. This route was followed by Pilkington, Hutton and Walker on the first ascent of this peak in 1883.

Where the Druim nan Ramh ridge abuts against the central peak the rocks are perpendicular and it is usual to traverse a ledge to the left to the gap between the central and west peaks; or, by scrambling up some easy rocks, a higher ledge can be reached which leads easily to the main ridge on the central peak well above the gap.

SGURR AN FHEADAIN (2215 feet)

This peak stands at the end of a long shoulder projecting from Bidean Druim nan Ramh into Coire na Creiche, and divides Coir' a' Mhadaidh from Tairneilear. The west face is cleft by the Waterpipe Gully, the chief feature of the mountain.

THE WATERPIPE GULLY 1300 feet VERY SEVERE

In the early ascents of this gully, several of the pitches were not taken direct but turned by traverses on the right walls. Today all the pitches, more than twenty of them, have been climbed direct, there being thus less severe alternatives either for the average party or as conditions permit.

A lengthy description is out of place here but some features can be given which are interesting. The first is a steep pitch of 80 feet just above the beginning of the gully. The second, about 300 feet up, is a crux pitch, a vertical one with a small waterfall. About midway between this pitch and the next feature at 850 feet up where the usual route goes up a broad chimney on the right there is a very thin overhanging one on the left (this is on the direct line). Climb this chimney by bridging (facing right). This leads to easier ground for 20 feet. The chimney narrows considerably and the next 20 feet to the exit is very severe. This pitch is 60/70 feet high. At 850 feet a stack of rock divides the gully— the stack can be followed direct. Finally near the top where the gully is narrow and the walls unclimbable, there is a hopeless pitch of about 60 feet. The route goes up a chimney in the left-hand corner of the pitch, and round a projecting rib of rock where the route regains the main gully.

First ascent by J. Kelsall and A. W. Hallitt in 1895.

The buttresses on either side of the gully give interesting scrambles.

THE SPUR AND SUMMIT GULLIES Moderate

On the north buttress starting some distance above the screes the first pitch is capped by a large rounded boulder prominent from the foot of the climb. Above this the gully is deeply cut and gives quite a good climb.

There is another gully further to the north in the same buttress, containing three good pitches, one quite stiff.

First ascent by A. P. Abraham, G. Bartrum, A. H. Binns and H. Harland in 1907.

COIRE TAIRNEILEAR—THE SLABS

The slabs rising from the head of Tairneilear to the Bealach na Glaic Moire are cleft by three gullies, clearly visible to anyone approaching from Coire na Creiche.

NORTH GULLY   Moderate

Can be used as an alternative to the ascent to the Bealach via the Stone Shoot. The first obstacle is an overhanging slab extending across the gully—avoid by a crack on left-hand wall. The final cave pitch gives a through route.

First ascent by H. Bishop, H. P. Cain and C. D. Yeomans in 1914.

CENTRE GULLY   300 feet   DIFFICULT

The high first pitch is the best of the climb and is overcome by bridging. Thereafter the gully becomes shallow and its angle lessens until, after a few pitches, definite climbing ends at mid-height on the slabs.

First ascent by H. G. Nicol, I. H. Oliver and A. Grieve on 15th September 1952.

SOUTH GULLY   700 feet   SEVERE

This gully is quite a different proposition from the other two and is probably almost a perfect gully.

Up to pitch 7 or 8 the standard is D.-V.D. Then a big pitch 60 feet with, in dry conditions, a beautiful greenish blue pool at its foot, difficult to pass. This pitch can be climbed direct, but in unfavourable conditions, there is a fine 70-foot very difficult pitch on the right wall starting at the outer tip of the pool (by W. D. Brooker). The following pitch has not been done direct but on the right wall climbing out on to the slabs and then back into the gully.

There follow some difficult pitches then the final chasm 60 feet by backing up past two chockstones—smooth walls.

First ascent by W. M. MacKenzie, A. M. MacAlpine and F. A. Oxley in July 1937.

D

SGURR A' MHADAIDH (3010 feet)

This is a fine mountain and consists of a series of peaks. It has fine cliffs falling into Coire Tairneilear and the corries at its eastern base.

The crossing of the four peaks, the south-west being the highest, is easier going from south-west to north-east than in the opposite direction. The only obstacles are on the second and third pinnacles.

The ascent is easily made by the Thuilm ridge from the col between Thuilm and Mhadaidh. Also from the head of Tairneilear by the "Foxes' Rake" which runs on to the final rocks of the Thuilm ridge.

There is another easy route, the Upper Rake, above and parallel with Foxes' Rake with finish between the third and fourth peaks (the highest).

TAIRNEILEAR FACE

NORTH-WEST BUTTRESS
1200 feet   VERY DIFFICULT

The buttress is in three sections of nearly equal height, the lowest and top sections being easy. Steep pitch in middle section can be turned on right by shallow gully; climb 50/60 feet then traverse back to middle line of buttress by narrow groove (60 feet).

First ascent by Dr J. N. Collie and party in 1896.

GAUGER'S GULLY   DIFFICULT

From the Upper Rake a deeply cut gully in the middle of the second peak. The gully consists of three pitches—the first is an easy scramble, the second is climbed on the left wall past a chockstone, and the third by backing up underneath a large chockstone.

First ascent by W. L. Woods, P. Greeman and W. H. Rae on 4th June 1939.

SHINING CLEFT   900 feet   MILD SEVERE

Start at the lowest point of the slabby rocks left of Slanting Gully and cross them to a cairn. Climb up to the right to a trap ledge, then up a 15-foot slab to a slanting chimney gap in a long low overhang. Slabs now lead right to a recess above the big cave in Slanting Gully. Cross the gully at this point. A small ledge runs easily up to the right for 200 feet, to a slabby depression topped by a basalt lip. The great V-Cleft is above, easy at first, then smooth and overhanging. Traverse right from the lip on to a ledge slanting up right to a short chimney and platform on the crest of the rib to the right of the Cleft. Then a chimney on the left, and steep rocks on the crest to Foxes' Rake near the finish of Archer Thomson's climb.

First ascent by G. H. Francis, J. F. Adams and E. A. Wrangham on 22nd June 1952.

FOXES' FOLLY   350 feet   SEVERE

An alternative to Slanting Gully when the latter is wet, and is on the buttress to its left.

Start from the base of obvious trap dyke 20 feet left of Slanting Gully, climbing the dyke to steeper rocks. A firm block belay is found near the gully (130 feet). Traverse up left until steep rocks can be climbed upwards to the right, leading to broken small overhang. Two small spike belays near. (35 feet.) Go up through overhang break above belay to steep slab leading to junction with Slanting Gully above wedged block. (30 feet.) Easy climbing on edge of gully to below final pitch below Foxes' Rake. (100 feet.) Use a crack to left of gully and reach the Rake. The climb then finishes up Slanting Gully. (50 feet.)

First ascent by D. Lever and A. Smee in July 1950.

SLANTING GULLY   700 feet   VERY DIFFICULT

The gully is in two sections. Foxes' Rake intersects rather more than half-way up. In the first section the second pitch, 80 feet, is passed by bridging or on the left by a narrow ledge. After crossing Foxes' Rake comes the "Cracks Pitch", the difficulty here being to get out of a small cave with an overhanging roof. The pitch can be avoided on the left. The final pitch—80 feet— V.D. The climb finishes on Upper Rake.

First ascent by A. P. Abraham, G. Bartrum, A. H. Binns and H. Harland in 1907.

TWO-PITCH GULLY   VERY DIFFICULT

This is a deep vertical chockstoned rift in the rock wall of the third peak and starts from the Upper Rake 100 yards to the right of Slanting Gully climb. The start is awkward as the gully does not come down to the screes.

First ascent by N. C. Madan and H. E. L. Porter in 1911.

FOX TRAP   200 feet   VERY DIFFICULT

On the south-west face of the third peak, starting from the Upper Rake to the right of Two-Pitch Gully. It is the narrow trap-dyke chimney, well seen from the south-west peak of Mhadaidh, slanting to the right. The chimney can easily be reached from the ridge by descending the rake leading into Tairneilear from the col between the third and south-west peaks, and is the first fault encountered on the way down. The route follows the chimney throughout, passing a few chockstones higher up, and finishes on the Main Ridge.

First ascent by C. M. Dixon and W. D. Brooker on 4th June 1951.

NORTH FACE OF SOUTH-WEST PEAK

ARCHER THOMSON'S ROUTE
900 feet   VERY DIFFICULT

Start about mid-way between Slanting and Deep Gash Gullies. Straightforward climb directly up the cliff to the summit.

First ascent by J. M. A. Thomson, H. O. Jones and L. G. Shadbolt in 1911.

PYE AND MALLORY'S ROUTE
900 feet   DIFFICULT

The start is similar to that of Thomson's route but at 30 feet traverse right upwards 150 feet, then 150 feet upwards slightly left continuing up to a large platform. Up 40 feet then left traverse to a curving chimney, finish the ascent of this on left wall. Easier climbing follows to the summit.

First ascent by D. R. Pye, G. H. L. Mallory, R. Mallory and L. G. Shadbolt in July 1918.

DEEP GASH GULLY   200 feet   VERY SEVERE

A cave with a mass of large chockstones jammed in the walls 30 feet up leaving an overhang of some 15 feet. Back up to the topmost chockstone, fix a sling and snaplink. The problem is now to use the sling for an outward lunge and to grasp a hand hold on the other side of the chockstone. The leader, when this is accomplished, has quite a struggle to stay put and at the same time insert his left foot in the sling. Once this is done the remainder of this pitch is straightforward (40 feet). Formidable overhang of about 25 feet on final section of next pitch. Back up for 25 feet where a running belay can be fixed. Use the sling as a hand hold and reverse position in

chimney. Chimney at this point 2-3 feet wide. Worm
outwards and upwards to edge of chimney where a
massive bollard can be grasped and a more orthodox
position can be reached and so to the top. (70 feet).
Two short pitches (V.D.), second one a left traverse, and
then a 40-foot overhanging chimney (S.). This is followed by a cave and chimney pitch, chimney very
severe. Narrow chimney with cutaway base. Descend
5 feet; climb up steep loose rocks on right wall until a
small jutting out piece of trap (shaky) is reached, from
here transfer to chimney. Arm pulls and knee jamming
to the top. (40 feet). Final three pitches straightforward.

First ascent by H. G. Nicol and A. S. Parker, 20th
September 1949.

COIR' AN UAIGNEIS FACE

Coir' an Uaigneis is the stony hollow lying high
across and between Sgurr a' Mhadaidh and Sgurr a'
Ghreadaidh on the Coruisk side.

SOUTH-EAST BUTTRESS (MAIN PEAK)
BROWN'S CLIMB   800 feet   DIFFICULT

This climb is on the left-hand side of the South-East
Buttress Gully. Straightforward buttress climb.

First ascent by W. Brown and party in 1897.

SOUTH-EAST BUTTRESS GULLY
800 feet   VERY DIFFICULT

This gully cuts the buttress into two. There are ten
pitches, the third of which is probably the hardest; above
this is a fine cave pitch with a through route. Above
pitch seven an escape can be made into Third/Fourth
Gully but go straight on. Near its termination the gully
forks—take the right one.

First ascent by E. W. Steeple and G. Barlow in 1910.

THIRD/FOURTH GULLY   MODERATE

Largely scree filled, one 50-foot pitch. Near the top gully branches, the right branch to the col between the two peaks; the left branch is a narrow chimney leading to the gap between the South-West Peak and a prominent pinnacle north of it.

SECOND/THIRD GULLY   460 feet   DIFFICULT

This commences near the bottom of a long rake which runs across the face of the Third Peak and the foot of the Second Peak. There are half a dozen pitches, the last being a large cave. The upper part is scree. It is possible to traverse into the upper part of First/Second Gully if a longer climb is desired.

First ascent by E. W. Steeple, G. Barlow and A. H. Doughty in 1913.

FIRST/SECOND GULLY   MODERATELY DIFFICULT

This is in two sections, the lower easy, the upper is deeply cut with three quite good pitches.

First ascent by Steeple and Barlow in 1913.

(The Peaks of Mhadaidh are numbered 1, 2, 3 and 4 —hence the naming of the gullies.)

SGURR A' GHREADAIDH (3190 feet)

Sgurr a' Ghreadaidh rises boldly at the head of Coruisk, and from the tourist viewpoint at the foot of the loch it is the most prominent peak.

WEST FACE

THE NORTH-WESTERN RIDGE OVER SGURR EADAR DA CHOIRE

In 1898 King, Gibbs and Dobson climbed this ridge, which is not difficult but affords plenty of scrambling.

The rotten rock at the foot can be avoided by traversing a rake from the scree below the Hidden Gully.

A good alternative is EAGLES' GULLY (Moderate), a long and narrow gully in the centre of the north face of Sgurr Eadar da Choire climbed in 1910 by Steeple, Barlow, Bowron and Doughty.

Both branches of Coire a' Ghreadaidh were descended from the top of Ghreadaidh early in its climbing history —the south branch by Collie and King so long ago as 1887.

HIDDEN GULLY   DIFFICULT

This gully is in the south branch of Coire a' Ghreadaidh. It cuts obliquely into the mountain and faces Sgurr Eadar da Choire. The climb is difficult to locate until one is near its foot. Chief features are first a large cave, a black chimney followed by a second cave, thereafter scrambling.

First ascent by F. Greig in 1908.

OVERHANGING GULLY
400/500 feet   VERY DIFFICULT

Ascend first two pitches of Hidden Gully as far as belay on chockstone at foot of wet chimney. Traverse left 20 feet and climb basalt dyke for some 80 feet. Continue up dyke using also left-hand gabbro wall for 100 feet. Go straight up gully to overhanging wall and cave. Climb right-hand of cave to a scoop. Climb scoop to large ledge. Climb finishes up gabbro ridge going over six-foot pinnacle.

First ascent by W. A. Greenwell and P. D. Roberts in July 1947.

VANISHING GULLY   Difficult

The next gully to the right of Hidden Gully, it contains several interesting pitches, but it becomes lost at about two-thirds of the height of the face.

First ascent by Barlow, Steeple, Doughty and Bowron in 1910.

DIAGONAL GULLY   Easy

Commences immediately below the Ghreadaidh—Thormaid col and leads diagonally up on to the Ghreadaidh ridge. It contains one pitch near the bottom which can be turned on the north side.

CORUISK FACE

The Terrace Buttress is divided in two by the Terrace Gully and the divisions are named the West and East Buttresses.

THE TERRACE, WEST BUTTRESS
1050 feet   Difficult

A start is made on steep rocks near the foot of the Terrace Gully. At 120 feet a difficult vertical section is encountered. Above this a stretch of open slabs leads to a gully or chimney sloping upwards to the left. This is followed to a shelf (400 feet). On the right a fine 80-foot wall leads to a ledge of shattered rock. A steep and rather difficult section of trap rock is succeeded by 100 feet or so of climbing on splendid rough gabbro. The total height of the Terrace is 650 feet.

Crossing the Terrace, a very narrow ledge running upwards to the Thormaid—Ghreadaidh gap is followed for some distance, until it threatens to become non-existent, then a trap chimney with a difficult pitch at the

top is climbed to more open ground above. The main
ridge is reached a short distance below the summit.

First ascent by E. W. Steeple and G. Barlow in July
1924.

THE TERRACE GULLY
600/700 feet   VERY DIFFICULT

This fine gully cuts through the southern rocks of
Ghreadaidh and faces Sgurr Coire an Lochain. A good
deal of water drains down this gully in wet weather.

The climb commences on a broad green ledge which
runs along the foot of the cliff above a low, vertical wall.
The first pitch is a deeply-cut cave. A ledge on the left
wall leads to an enclosed chimney, from which the
climber emerges through an aperture between the chock
stones. After surmounting two small obstacles, a wet
chockstone pitch is reached which is turned by the edge
of the buttress on the left. A short distance higher a fine
branch chimney rises on the right (no record of ascent).
A wet slippery pitch above the gully widens out below
a large formidable cave pitch, the foot of which is reached
by ascending waterworn slabs and a short scree slope.
From the foot of this slope the right wall is climbed to a
small resting place, from which an exposed traverse is
made upwards to the left to a recess beside the capstone.
This is difficult to enter, but the exit is easy. Above this
pitch is a long chimney containing an arched block.
This has not as yet been climbed; a narrow crack on the
right is climbed. Easy rocks now lead to a high chockstone pitch climbed on its left wall. A short scramble
leads to the Terrace.

First ascent by Steeple, Barlow and Doughty in
August 1920.

THE TERRACE, EAST BUTTRESS
600/700 feet   DIFFICULT

The climb commences at a little chimney near the east angle of the buttress. After ascending 120 feet, a grass patch is reached, from the upper limit of which a long chimney, bearing upwards to the left across the buttress, is climbed for 350 feet, when an exposed traverse is made along and up a vertical wall to a ledge. Steep rocks above the ledge lead to easy slabs, which are followed to the Terrace.

First ascent by Steeple and Barlow in 1922.

A suitable continuation for any of these climbs can be made by following a well marked rib in the centre of the Ghreadaidh face. By this means the main ridge is reached a few feet below the south summit, and 1600 feet from the foot of the buttress.

SOUTH-EAST RIDGE (COLLIE'S ROUTE)
2000 feet   DIFFICULT

Two prominent gullies meet higher up like an inverted U. The start is to the left of the left-hand branch. Follow the gully to beyond the junction with the other gully where it is possible to traverse diagonally leftwards (a walk) to a position where the south-west ridge can be reached and followed to the top.

First ascent by Professor Collie and E. B. Howell in 1896.

SOUTH-EAST RIDGE (DIRECT ROUTE)
1000 feet   DIFFICULT

The route commences some distance to the south of Collie's. The climb starts 20 yards to the left of a deeply cut gully and is marked by quite a prominent rowan tree. The route works diagonally upwards and to the left by steep pitches connecting a series of dyke-lines until the Terrace is reached. Finish by the south-east ridge.

First ascent by W. A. Morrison and D. H. Menzies in 1920.

SLAB ROUTE   900 feet   SEVERE

Two prominent gullies in the centre of the cliff meet higher up like an inverted U. The start is 20 feet to the right of the right-hand gully up the red slabs. After 100 feet the gully is climbed to a cave. A short, steep wall on the right is followed by easy rocks for about 150 feet, the gully is crossed and moderate slabs are followed for about 500 feet. Make for a large perched block on the skyline and pass it on to easy ground on either side. Walk up to the final cliff, and 50 feet to the right of a large black overhang is a slab slanting to the left above it, with a delicate traverse 45 feet up. After 150 feet a basalt wall is climbed to a large grass terrace. The final buttress is between two gullies. The base overhangs mostly, but a steep start is made on the left and loose rock follows until the buttress steepens to a tower. Start up a mantleshelf on the left and climb direct or by a traverse to the left to easy ground. Bad rock here enjoins great care. The final tower direct is severe under bad conditions.

First ascent by J. E. Byrom and P. Wigglesworth in June 1939.

CORUISK BUTTRESS   800 feet ap.   SEVERE

This stands up boldly to the right of Collie's route. A single line of weakness runs upwards obliquely from left to right. This determines the route. The start is at the lowest tongue of rock, about the centre. Traverse up left to main weakness and follow it diagonally right by steep grooves until checked by small overhang beneath a big black one at 200 feet. Escape on right and up more continuous grooves, one of the hardest moves on the route. Soon there is a smooth, vertical wall above and an overhang below. The next crux occurs at 400 feet. Continue on the same line until it seems possible to traverse off the face, instead of which climb for 200 feet or so the first easy crack going straight up. The climb is severe, with high angle and continuous difficulty.

First ascent by C. M. G. Smith and R. C. Putman.

EAG DUBH GULLY   DIFFICULT

This leads up to the gap of An Dorus from the Coruisk side. It contains eight or nine pitches, one about midway is difficult. A scree shoot above leads to An Dorus Gap, south of Eag Dubh.

First ascent by Steeple, Barlow and Doughty in 1913.

SGURR THORMAID (3040 feet)

The traverse of the ridge line offers no difficulty, the three small teeth north of the summit being easily turned on the west.

SGURR NA BANACHDICH (3167 feet)

The main ridge of Banachdich is well broken up but the gaps are easily passed. The Bealach Coire na Banachdich is easily reached from Coruisk but from Glen Brittle the way lies up a scree gully on the Dearg slopes quite off the direct route to the Bealach.

The ridge of An Diallaid is easy if the line of least resistance is followed.

AN DIALLAID

THE BRANCHING GULLY   Difficult

This is the prominent gully which faces north-west across Glen Brittle, having two branches on the south side. It contains eight pitches, of which the upper three are difficult.

First ascent by W. Garden, J. R. Levack and W. A. Reid in September 1908.

NORTH-EAST GULLY   300 feet   Difficult

This is a deep, narrow gully, which slopes up obliquely to the left and contains about seven pitches.

First ascent by P. M. Barclay and J. A. Ramsay in July 1929.

BANACHDICH GULLY   150 feet   Difficult

The head of Coire na Banachdich is a semi-circular wall of rock in the centre of which is a black deeply-cut gully. There are four pitches, the top one is the best.

First ascent by G. B. Gibbs, W. W. King and John MacKenzie in 1898.

The rocks on both sides of the gully are good and give nice climbing.

SGURR NAN GOBHAR (2047 feet)

From the summit of the North Peak of Banachdich a long ridge runs off to the west, terminating at a cairn, 2047 feet.

GOAT'S GULLY
700 feet ap.   Moderate to Difficult

This gully, the conspicuous black gash on the south flank of Sgurr nan Gobhar, makes a pleasant climb for an "off day". In the lower half of the gully there is a lot of loose scree. About mid-way one pitch has quite a good through route and the top pitch may be difficult.

First recorded by T. Shaw and C. M. Dixon on 9th August 1950.

COIREACHAN RUADH FACE
THE TWINS

Just to the north of Bealach Coire na Banachdich lie two prominent steep buttresses divided by a dark gully.

SOUTH TWIN   250 feet   MODERATELY DIFFICULT

The foot is a huge slab topped by overhang. On the left flank, however, a chimney cuts into the buttress and the right edge of this gives steep but not difficult climbing to a level crest. From here trend left across a wall and then up the crest to the summit. Rock rather shattered.

NORTH TWIN   350 feet   MILD SEVERE

From a recessed platform 20 feet up, a steep crack is climbed to a ledge on the left flank. From the far end of this ledge, the steep slabby left wall of the buttress is climbed until possible to traverse right to the crest. A vertical knife edge leads up on good holds to a level arête of solid rock ending in a neck. Above this the rock becomes rather shattered.

MIDGET RIDGE   400 feet   MODERATE

From the Bealach Coire na Banachdich the Main Ridge leading north goes over a minor summit housing the Twins and then descends a very little to an incipient col. From this col easy ground leads down to a level scree terrace running below the summit cliffs of Banachdich. Traversing this one passes below steep black cliffs cut by terraces till a prominent narrow arête is reached trending slightly right. The crest is followed closely and gives very pleasant climbing on good rock, at times narrowing to a knife edge.

THE CLOUDED BUTTRESS
600 feet   MILD SEVERE

About 100 yards north of Midget Ridge, beyond a stretch of imposing vertical walls and just to the right of a big gully lies this prominent buttress. It ascends directly towards the main summit of Banachdich. There appears to be only one possible route and the rock tends to slope outwards. In places it must be carefully treated.

From the foot trend first right and then left. Then steep slabs are crossed towards the left until possible to climb upwards. Work right and upwards to a slabby ledge. Now traverse left on slabs to a shallow chimney 10 feet high and then left and up to a recess in the left hand corner of the buttress at a great white scar. Exit from recess by the right hand corner (crux) and thence straight up for over 100 feet to a terrace. The final tower above may be avoided but gives a pleasant finish to the climb, just a little to the south of the Banachdich summit.

These four routes were all ascended by T. W. Patey and W. D. Brooker on 15th August 1953.

SGURR DEARG (3206 feet)

THE WINDOW BUTTRESS   300 feet   DIFFICULT

Half-way up the south side of Coire na Banachdich there is a tower with a window in it. When looking up the corrie the Window Buttress is seen in profile. The climb starts at the foot of the rocks. The start now usually followed is by a steep 100 foot crack (very difficult—R. C. Evans in 1938) some 12 yards to the left of the original start. The remainder of the climb is easily followed.

First ascent by Professor Collie in 1906.

It is possible to climb the buttress by the interesting arête which bounds the steep gully separating the buttress from the main mass of the mountain.

BISHOP'S CLIMB   DIFFICULT

There is also a climb on the next mass of rock to the east, starting on a level with the top of the Window Tower. A cairn at the foot of a 20-foot gully with a wedged chockstone at the top marks the beginning of the route.

First ascent by H. Bishop and C. D. Yeomans in 1914.

TOOLIE GROOVES   300 feet   HARD SEVERE

High above the Window Buttress is another buttress which is marked by a conspicuous black chimney. This chimney in its lower reaches becomes a groove. Start here.

Climb groove, with very difficult start then up for 80 feet. Exit via an obvious gangway on the left to a platform, then up a corner to a similar platform.

From highest point, climb until final overhang overawes, move right, where a fine mantleshelf leads to the base of a steep little slab; climb this and notch in overhang (100 feet).

Finish by little crack on the right.

First ascent by J. R. Marshall, C. L. Donaldson and G. Hood in June 1953.

E

BLACK CHIMNEY   DIFFICULT

This is in the prominent buttress high up in Coire na Banachdich to the east of Window Buttress.

First ascent by G. Barlow and party in 1909.

INACCESSIBLE PINNACLE

The Pinnacle projects from the south-east side of the summit, which it overtops by some 20 feet. It is most easily reached by a stone shoot from the head of Coire Lagan or by the western shoulder of Sgurr Dearg.

EAST RIDGE   125 feet   MODERATE

First ascent by C. L. Pilkington on 18th August 1880.

WEST RIDGE   40 feet   DIFFICULT

The only difficulty consists in getting from a narrow ledge up a 5-foot rise to a sloping platform.

First ascent by A. H. Stocker and A. G. Parker in 1886.

NORTH-WEST CORNER   DIFFICULT

Start from the screes 10 feet from the usual western route, climb the prominent crack which runs up for a considerable distance along the edge of the north face.

First ascent by H. Raeburn.

THE SOUTH CRACK   MILD SEVERE

The long crack or chimney in the middle of the south face of the Pinnacle, although comparatively short, requires a good deal of muscular effort. There is a bulge about 30 feet up when the climber is forced out of the crack. At one or two places the crack is very narrow.

THE SOUTH FACE CLIMBS
(1)   VERY SEVERE

Commence a few feet to the left of the crack. An upward movement left to a small ledge. Forty feet higher a second ledge, step right into a corner and finish directly up the face.

(2)   VERY SEVERE

Is a little further left joining the former route at a ledge below the summit ridge.

First ascent by Piggott and Wilding in 1921.

AN STAC

This is the bold buttress under the Inaccessible Pinnacle which projects from Sgurr Dearg in the direction of Sgurr Mhic Coinnich. It was descended in 1891 by Gibson, Morse and Wicks.

THE AN STAC CHIMNEY
200 feet   MODERATE

This is a line of a trap-dyke and ends under the summit of the buttress.

First ascent by Goggs and Russell in 1908.

SOUTH BUTTRESS

This triangular-faced buttress looks across the head of Coire Lagan, height approximately 600 feet.

SOUTH FACE—BALY'S ROUTE
MODERATELY DIFFICULT

A gully adjoins the buttress on the west. Ascend this for 150 feet, afterwards follow the buttress on the right.

First ascent by Professor E. C. C. Baly in 1909.

WESTERN DRAINPIPE RIDGE
480 feet   SEVERE

Start at a cairn at the foot on the right (facing) ridge of the gully. The line of this rib is held all the way, with only minor deviations, over a succession of slabs and walls. The crux occurs at 100 feet from the start, when a hard move up and left is made with the aid of a piton.

First ascent by P. G. White, T. W. Waghorn and C. J. Breeze on 25th August 1952.

BARBER'S ROUTE   210 feet   VERY DIFFICULT

This climb lies between Baly's and Central Routes. From cairn on large grass terrace to a sentry-box with belay (30 feet). Ascend chimney 10 feet to a sloping ledge on the right, then by a difficult movement to a steep, narrow groove, and so to a small stance (60 feet). Ascend left wall of groove 25 feet, then by a flake, cross this to the right wall and climb to a large platform on right (60 feet). Follow the groove for 30 feet and finish by 30 feet at an easier angle (60 feet). Several lines of weakness may now be followed to the summit ridge.

First ascent by B. K. Barber, M. Burton, G. Eisig and H. B. Law on 2nd August 1937.

CENTRAL ROUTE   250 feet   SEVERE

This route lies on the centre of the Southern Buttress to the right of Barber's route and to the left of Steeple and Barlow's route.

The start lies in a corner at the centre of the wide sloping, grassy terrace which lies immediately above the introductory rocks. The first pitches of this climb follow the line of an obvious and impressive fault in the steep lower part of the buttress. The first pitch is the hardest; escape by a shelf on the left is possible at 20 feet, but the route continues up on the right over a steep slab forming a corner with the vertical wall on the left (belay at 50 feet). The next pitch zig-zags by slabs, a chimney and a groove to a broken recess; whence another 50 feet by a corner and an overhanging chimney lead to the foot of a steep and obvious trap chimney rising to the right. Above this last obstacle easier rocks lead to the arête connecting the buttress to the mountain itself.

First ascent by D. D. Stewart and D. N. Mill on 15th July 1950.

LAGAN ROUTE   280 feet   SEVERE

Towards the eastern corner of the buttress is a spring with a green mossy patch and 20 yards to the right in a raised alcove is a dyke with a crack on its left.

Follow crack for 20 feet then traverse right across dyke to a flake; go up it onto slabs above where there is a belay (60 feet). Climb in easy chimney on the left. Go left for a few feet to a perched block; slip off block and climb slabs above to the left of an inverted flake to a grassy recess and ledge (60 feet). Go up groove above ledge then bear right to climb slabs on small holds.

First ascent by D. Thomas and G. Goddard in August 1947.

EAST CORNER   MODERATELY DIFFICULT

From the east corner of the buttress moderate rocks can be followed to the top of the buttress.

First ascent by Steeple and Barlow in 1912.

WEST FACE OF SOUTH BUTTRESS
MISTAKEN CRACK   200 feet   HARD SEVERE

Two obvious chimneys in the high upper left-hand corner of the west face of South Buttress—take the right-hand one.

Ascend chimney to overhanging block, pass on left wall (60 feet). Climb wall close to and left of crack, pass chockstone to a stance (70 feet). Pass another chockstone into a small cave. Climb left wall from cave (20 feet).

First ascent by G. S. Beattie, W. K. Davies and K. A. Sturrock on 29th July 1955.

COIREACHAN RUADHA FACE
O'BRIEN AND JULIAN'S CLIMB
300 feet ap.   VERY DIFFICULT

Starting from the screes, 70 feet of steep rocks on left wall of a conspicuous cave are mounted, and then easier rocks lead to the lower of the two prominent terraces which cross this face. Between the terraces the climbing is difficult. Finally the north-north-east ridge is gained just above a striking rock tower. The rocks are wet and slippery.

First ascent by Conor O'Brien and E. L. Julian in 1912.

THE BUTTRESS BETWEEN BEALACH COIRE LAGAN AND THE 2595 COL ON THE CORUISK SIDE

This buttress has been named the *Bealach Buttress* and so far there are seven routes on it. The gully from col 2595 appears to offer a means of approach to the foot of the buttress, that is from the Coire Lagan side. This gully has been named "Rotten Gully" and the climber can gather from that the nature of the terrain. Descend the gully to the Terrace which runs from the Bealach Buttress under the Coireachan Ruadha cliffs of Sgurr Mhic Coinnich. The descent of the cliff below the Terrace starts just to the true left of Rotten Gully down a little chimney and thence by easier ground to the screes.

The best approach is to leave the main ridge at the true Bealach Coire Lagan, 2655 feet, and scramble down loose grass and boulder slopes, passing many outcropping basalt dykes, descending first rightwards (southwards) then back left (northwards) and down a 6-ft. rock wall on to a scree fan. From the ridge do not follow the actual screes, as they lead too far under An Stac. Once on the scree fan, traverse southwards across scree, under broken rocky slopes, descending gradually until on the Terrace which sweeps round Bealach Buttress. From here climb down to the foot of the Arrowhead.

LOST ARROW   350 feet   VERY SEVERE

There are four main pitches—all serious. Climb the centre chimney of the Arrowhead, past a few awkward chockstones, and climb the final few feet on the left wall. Cross the Terrace to the same fault which continues as an easy grassy, broad crack for about 80 feet. Cross The Bow, until a belay in a wet cave in the steeper chimney above is reached (80 feet). Up the chimney, usually mossy and wet, to a belay in a cave below a large pointed chockstone (60 feet). Climb down, out, and round the chockstone, and over it to the foot of another overhanging section (30 feet). Climb the overhang above on the left and continue to the top of the crack (50 feet). The fault-line finishes on the grassy Upper Terrace near the start of the easy crack at the top of The Bow. It is possible to finish by climbing this, or to climb the face straight ahead. This gives some good climbing on friable rock with some unexpectedly awkward moves. Scrambling leads to the summit. A route of character. Needs dry weather. Can be climbed in nails.

First ascent by C. M. Dixon and J. E. Monk on 4th June 1954.

THE BOW   350 feet   MILD VERY SEVERE

Start—the right-hand crack of the Arrowhead. Pleasant climbing using the crack and slab on the right. Walk across the Terrace to the right-hand of two faults which cross the cliff above (60 feet). A short steep chimney—greasy. Follow the fault, crossing Lost Arrow, to where it becomes an overhanging crack which bifurcates higher up and leads to a large isolated slab (40 feet). Climb this crack. Hard (50 feet). Continue pleasantly up the slab by the crack in its right corner, which steepens near the top (70 feet). Scramble to the Upper Terrace, with the deep-cut section of Hourglass Crack nearby on the left, passing a weird rock bridge on the left (100 feet). Climb the broad easy-angled crack above the Upper Terrace to the top (150 feet). A pleasant route as a whole, with one very exacting pitch. A climb suited for vibrams.

First ascent by C. M. Dixon and J. E. Monk on 4th June 1954.

HOURGLASS CRACK   500 feet   HARD SEVERE

There are sheer uninviting cliffs on the south face of the buttress, while the east flank is broken and easy angled, but the corner where the two faces join offers interest to the climber. Hourglass Crack is on this section and gives many varieties of chimney and crack climbing, with a crux similar to that on the South Crack on the Inaccessible Pinnacle, but harder.

Start from the screes where three cracks form a down-pointing arrowhead. Climb the left one to a broad terrace which crosses the face. Behind the terrace, and a little to the left, another crack leads up a steep wall. It is the true continuation of the lower left-hand crack of the arrowhead. The crack forces the climber outside where it narrows; this is the crux. Above this it enters an impressive section, deeply cut with steep sides, leading easily over a few small pitches to a huge overhanging cave. Climb the right wall on small holds or back up between the walls to pass the cave. This is an unusual and enjoyable pitch, with fine views of Sgurr Coire an Lochain. The wide crack continues to the final cave. Back out of this, then cross to the left wall and climb on to the buttress to the left of the overhang, whence an easy scramble leads to the ridge.

First ascent by C. M. Dixon and T. Shaw on 7th August 1950.

GEMINI   500 feet   VERY SEVERE

Start immediately to the right of a shallow broken groove on the flat face to the right of the Arrowhead recess. Cairn. Pleasant climbing up the slabby face to the right of the groove leads in 150 feet to the Terrace, with belays at intervals. Cross the Terrace, to use an inserted chockstone belay in a crack in a corner. Start climbing 15 feet to the right of this crack, following an obvious rightward rising traverse, then back leftwards to a small terrace, after 100 feet of severe climbing. The next 100 feet is the most exacting section. From two shaky pinnacles step on to the face and climb to the foot of a steep groove; traverse right on to twin cracks (visible from the screes below) on the steep section of the face. Climb the right-hand crack with difficulty to an easier section, then up the left-hand crack to a belay on the left. A good 60-foot pitch follows. Climb the pinnacle immediately above the belay to its top, then up the face beyond to the top of the right-hand of twin pinnacles and up over another pinnacle to the Upper

Terrace. A hundred feet of easy climbing up the buttress above leads to the summit slopes. Clean, rough rock.

First ascent by C. M. Dixon and R. Cra'ster, through leads, on 5th June 1954.

PINNACLE FACE   450 feet   SEVERE

A very pleasant route on clean rock. The climb aims for a pinnacle on the face of Bealach Buttress. Start at a cairn on the screes, half-way between the foot of the Arrowhead and Black Cleft. A hundred feet of easy climbing, following a shallow small crack, leads to the Terrace. Climb the clean crack in the face above, runners available, then traverse rightwards across the foot of the Pinnacle to a stance in its right corner. From the top of the Pinnacle, step back left into the crack and up it to a ledge, then up the easier face of the buttress above, across a grass patch and up the short steeper wall behind, climbing to the right of a basalt fault. This leads to the Upper Terrace, after about 200 feet of climbing from the Pinnacle. The steep wall above is not climbed direct, but its edge about 40 feet to the right gives pleasant climbing to the summit slopes.

First ascent by R. Cra'ster and C. M. Dixon, through leads, on 5th June 1954.

BLACK CLEFT   400 feet   VERY SEVERE

The route follows the deeply cut crack or chimney which separates the other climbs of Bealach Buttress from the "unclimbable" wall on the left. Start from the screes at the foot of the cleft, below the Terrace (which is almost non-existent on this part of the cliff). The first 80 feet gives easy scrambling with a little chockstone pitch leading to a platform. Climb the steep narrow awkward chimney above, passing a chockstone at 25 feet, to ledge at 50 feet. The chimney above is steep, but climb the broken wall on the immediate left. Steep, delicate climbing on loose rock for about 50 feet, then follow an easier section which steepens after 40 feet, going over an awkward slab in the chimney to the foot of a small chockstone overhang. It is possible to escape from the cleft hereabouts, towards the Upper Terrace on the right, but once embarked on, the upper section allows no escape. Climb the overhang above to a jammed block belay, whence another short strenuous overhang is surmounted. Continue up the chimney over a large doubtful jammed block to a chockstone in the recesses of the cleft. A final steep 60-foot pitch goes straight up the steep chimney ahead until it is possible to climb out on the left wall and up to the top. A strenuous and exacting route. Every pitch has interest and severity.

First ascent by C. M. Dixon and J. E. Monk on 3rd June 1954.

THUNDERBOLT SHELF 500 feet VERY DIFFICULT

The south flank of Bealach Buttress is formed by a gigantic vertical wall. The route is on the face immediately to the left of this wall and keeps close to it.

The lower part consists of three almost vertical walls each about 60 feet high. The first is turned by climbing up a huge chimney cleaving the south flank of the Bealach Buttress. From the chimney traverse left along a ledge for 30 feet and climb the wall above to another ledge. Move left for 15 feet and climb the third tier to a ledge which is actually the continuation of the Terrace (on Mhic Coinnich).

The route now slants up to the left keeping fairly close to the wall on the right and one pitch goes over a huge semi-detached flake on the wall itself.

Higher up a direct upward line is taken finishing by a prominent vertical chimney which leads to the main ridge some 100 feet or so from the 2595 col.

First ascent by T. W. Patey and W. D. Brooker on 13th August 1953.

SGURR MHIC COINNICH (3107 feet)

The long back of this mountain is one of the sharpest ridges in the Cuillin and offers an easy approach from the Bealach Coire Lagan. Immediately beyond the summit on its south side the main ridge drops precipitously to the Mhic Coinnich—Thearlaich col. The gap can be reached quite readily from the corries on either side.

On the precipitous south end of Mhic Coinnich there are several cracks and chimneys. In the middle is King's Chimney which gives the most sporting route to the summit.

KING'S CHIMNEY   DIFFICULT

The chimney starts about 60 feet above the col and is reached by an easy scramble. The middle part is steep and the overhanging top of the chimney is avoided by a short traverse across a steep and smooth slab on the right.

First ascent by W. W. King and party in 1898.

COLLIE'S LEDGE   MODERATE

Professor Collie in 1890 made a way up to the left of King's Chimney by following an obvious ledge 20 feet above the col and without difficulty the ledge can be followed round on to the Coire Lagan face and the ridge can be gained north of the summit. From the ledge the summit can be gained by short steep climbs no harder than difficult.

WEST BUTTRESS

1000 feet   DIFFICULT

This buttress running up from Coire Lagan gives a good climb. If the middle line of the buttress is followed there are some good pitches in the lower section; the middle is easy and the upper part, which is more defined, has a fine chimney.

JEFFREY'S DYKE

1000 feet   MODERATELY DIFFICULT

This is the most continuous trap dyke to the left of the long West Buttress which reaches down from the summit to the screes above the lochan.

Start up slabby bulge above screes and continue over moderate rocks for 150 to 200 feet to foot of groove or dyke line. Keep to this groove, with occasional recourse to the walls. About 50 feet up is a grass terrace. Cross this and climb straight on to another grass terrace. Move a few yards to the right along this terrace and again go straight up steep rocks, soon traversing obliquely back to the left and upwards over the rim of a steep part to a little mossy terrace. Go a few steps to the right and about 15 feet up a deep narrow cleft and attain Collie's Ledge. Cross it and climb a 20-foot wall on small holds to the summit ridge.

First ascent by R. Jeffrey, Mrs Jeffrey, J. H. B. Bell, Mrs Bell and C. M. Allan, on 24th May 1948.

COIREACHAN RUADHA FACE

This face can be traversed by an easy rake running up from left to right, leading to the north end of the summit ridge.

The following four climbs, omitting North-East Gully, on the Coireachan Ruadha face of Mhic Coinnich were first ascended by W. D. Brooker and C. M. Dixon.

THE NORTH-EAST BUTTRESS
350 feet   DIFFICULT

This buttress lies immediately to the right of N.E. Gully. Start at the side near the gully, and from the cairn climb a series of broken walls and corners. At nearly 200 feet comes a short steep pitch (good holds), followed by a shelf with an awkward wall at its back. Climb this, then climb the steep wall above by a 50-foot crack on the left. The crack slants back to the right, and from it an easy slab leads to the neck of the buttress, where the N.E. Gully and the small gully on the right join. Above, a steep final wall leads to the ridge. Start the wall on the left, then trend up and rightwards to the ridge.—24th July 1950.

NORTH-EAST GULLY   350/400 feet   HARD SEVERE

This is a conspicuous gully on the right of this face.

After almost 200 feet of difficult climbing a large flake on the right can be ascended and the right traverse across its top is exposed, almost severe. From a stance at the end of this traverse one climbs up a groove for a few feet and then moves left across and up the steep broad rib. There is a delicate hard severe move here but the difficulties are over as a groove slanting up to the right leads easily to a broken platform some 40 feet below the ridge of Sgurr Mhic Coinnich.

First ascent by C. O'Brien and E. L. Julian in 1912.

THE FLUTED BUTTRESS   700 feet   HARD SEVERE

The broad buttress on the Coireachan Ruadha face of the peak, lying just to the left of the N.E. Gully. A series of overhangs about 200 feet up the buttress, broken into three fins or flutes, is a conspicuous feature. Start at a cairn on the Terrace, near the centre of the buttress and to the right of a huge right-angled corner. Climb a little rib for 25 feet (belay); then traverse right under an overhang for 50 feet, when the overhang can be climbed to a ledge above. Follow the ledge to the right, then up into an easy-angled chimney. Climb this to where it steepens under the flutes and traverse out to the right on to a slab, the gangway, below a huge overhang. Follow the rightward trend of the slab, with the overhanging flute on the left and the wall of the buttress dropping into the N.E. Gully on the right, until it steepens; then traverse out on the wall on the right. Delicate and very exposed climbing leads to the right and up to the easement above the overhangs. Follow a broken groove up the easement, trending back left to the centre of the buttress, and climb a short groove to a small terrace with a cairn on its left edge. From here the "Escape Route" continues the original plan of finding the easiest route up the buttress. This lies up a crack on the right-hand edge of the slabs to the right, and soon leads to the summit ridge of the peak; it is never more than difficult. The true and best finish to the climb lies up the little rib on the left of the cairn on the terrace. Climb the rib, following the line of a crack up its crest, till it steepens and ends on a ledge below a stupendous overhanging nose split by a crack. Attack the wall on the right by a hard crack in a groove. Step left to a ledge, then back right up an easy groove. From the recess at the top of the groove traverse right to a ledge, and along it, moving up and rightwards over two little corners, to end at a cairn on the ridge. A good face climb of continuous severity.—1st August 1950.

THE CRACK OF DAWN   600 feet   VERY SEVERE

The climb lies on the Fluted Buttress. The first 200 feet go up the S.E. wall of the buttress, then the crack trends leftward across the front of the buttress and finishes on the crack followed by the "Escape Route" of the Fluted Buttress route. Start at the foot of the crack (cairn) about 50 yards left of the start of F.B. route, at the corner where the S.E. wall joins the front wall of the buttress. Climb the crack for 80 feet to a niche offering a stance, with a delicate move at about 60 feet. Climb out of the niche up the overhanging crack above for a few feet, then traverse on to the exposed wall on the right and up to the platform which crosses the face at this point. Climb the steep chimney directly above to the top of the S.E. wall, then follow the easier-angled crack which now slants across the face, to where its line becomes indefinite (cairn). Climb the steep short crack immediately to the left of a little rib of clean rough rock, and near the top of the crack move to the right across the rib itself, passing a big rock flake; then climb up to the terrace and cairn on the F.B. route. The Crack finishes up the slabs on the right, taking exactly the same line as the Escape Route on F.B. The Crack of Dawn follows steep, clean and sound rock, and the severity of the lower section is continuous. The climb is probably the hardest route in Skye at present. A rubber climb for dry conditions.—6th August 1951.

FORGOTTEN GROOVE   250 feet   VERY DIFFICULT

This climb lies on the face of the peak, immediately below the summit cairn. The groove, formed by a slab on the left and a vertical bounding wall on the right, is well seen from the west ridge of Sgurr Coire an Lochain. Approach the groove by easy scrambling from near the foot of the Easy Rake. The lower part of the groove is very steep, and is climbed by a thin crack in the corner of the groove. Enter the steep crack at the foot by climbing a short way up the slab on the left and traversing in, but the crack can be entered direct. Follow the crack up the groove; the angle gradually eases and the groove finishes after 200 feet. From here tricky climbing over friable rock leads to the broken rocks below the summit cairn.—12th August 1951.

SGURR COIRE AN LOCHAN (2480 feet)

The East Ridge of Sgurr Thearlaich connects this mountain with the Main Ridge.

In 1896 Collie, Howell and Naismith with John Mackenzie made probably the first ascent of this summit. Their route lay over the north face giving them almost a thousand feet of rock-climbing mostly on steep smooth slabs. There is no recorded description of this climb and indeed the nature of this face makes it difficult to give one that can be easily followed. There is certainly a mountaineering flavour about the climbing here.

RAEBURN'S ROUTE   1000 feet   VERY DIFFICULT

Start below the overhang of the very steep edge facing Bidein. After a few hundred feet a traverse is forced on steep slabs round to the east. There doesn't appear to be any way through the overhang till right on the other corner of the tower facing the head of Coruisk.

First ascent by H. Raeburn, J. B. Meldrum and the brothers Wallwork in 1913.

SHELF ROUTE   500 feet ap.   SEVERE

Seen from Druim nan Ramh in morning light, an inclined shelf, nearly 300 feet long, is visible. It starts as a 5-foot ledge, broadens to a sweep of slabs 30 to 40 feet high, and lies just above the overhanging part of the north face. It can be approached from below by a line of weakness from the right to left, which continues beyond the shelf. The shelf slopes from left to right, and

F

the only practicable escape appears to be from its
extreme right edge up steep rocks for about 60 feet to the
easier rocks near the summit.

Start by a traverse from the right, but could be from
directly below. The shelf is reached 150 feet above the
start or 250 feet from the lowest rocks, and is climbed in
three pitches, each requiring a runout of 110 feet.
Difficulty gradually increases, especially when rounding
a corner beyond which the shelf broadens out, where
slabs are hard and smooth with few positive holds.
Rubbers or stockings are best. From the top of the slabs
an easy traverse leads to broken rocks at right end of
shelf. Climb steep and difficult rocks directly for 40 feet
to a ledge and block belay. The route goes up a 20-foot
wall of slabs to the right and another short wall, thereafter scrambling on the north ridge leads to the summit.
On the hard parts belays are scarce.

First ascent by J. D. G. Davidson and F. R. Brooke
on 23rd October 1949.

SGURR THEARLAICH (3201 feet)

To follow the ridge line from the Mhic Coinnich Col
over Sgurr Thearlaich to the Stone Shoot and Sgurr
Alasdair is an interesting but easy scramble.

The south-east ridge of Sgurr Thearlaich running to
Sgurr Dubh contains the well-known Thearlaich-Dubh
Gap. The gap was first crossed by Collie and King in
1891. The wall on the Thearlaich side is about 80 feet
high; on the other 30 feet, and both are difficult perhaps
more so as the rocks are now worn very smooth. The
gap is easily reached from the Ghrunnda side.

Beyond the gap there is a sharp descent of the rocks
of the Pinnacle where care has to be taken. A short
distance further is the Bealach Coir' an Lochain.

QUIVER   250 feet   SEVERE

The route is on Ghrunnda face of pinnacled south wall of Thearlaich-Dubh Gap. Climb steep cracks, a few feet to the right of prominent right-angled corner at foot of the pinnacle. Traverse left above the corner before climbing a steep and severe wall on small holds. Easier but less reliable rocks lead to the top of the pinnacle by its left edge.

First ascent by J. Hammond and R. Morden on 16th May 1951.

BOWER'S CLIMB   VERY DIFFICULT

Climb the first pitch of the Thearlaich-Dubh Gap (Ghrunnda side), then traverse round corner on left— 70 feet. The open face is then climbed for 250/300 feet. The climb ends near the head of the Stone Shoot.

First ascent by G. S. Bower and J. B. Meldrum in 1919.

The west side of Sgurr Thearlaich contains five gullies which run down into the Alasdair Stone Shoot. They are named A, B, C, D and E going from north to south.

GULLY A   MODERATELY DIFFICULT

A narrow cave pitch ascended on left-hand wall, through a tunnel into an enclosed chimney. Climb this for 30 feet then a chockstone pitch and finally a narrow chimney.

First ascent by Steeple, Barlow and Doughty in 1908.

GULLY B   DIFFICULT

Three easy pitches and then a good 60-foot chimney.

GULLY C   DIFFICULT

A deep fissure with jammed blocks at the top followed by a cave with a through route.

GULLY D   VERY DIFFICULT

The best pitch is one of 100 feet near the top.

First ascent of Gullies B, C and D by Buckle, Barlow and Doughty in 1908.

GULLY E

This gully is more open but has probably not been entirely climbed. Slabby rocks on the right (difficult) are the usual finish.

Pilkington probably followed this route in making the first ascent of the mountain in 1880.

EAST RIDGE   MODERATE

Its ascent is probably the quickest way of reaching the summit from Coir' an Lochain. The ridge is steep but broken.

First ascent by H. Raeburn and party in 1913.

SGURR ALASDAIR (3251 feet)

The highest of the Cuillin and one of the most graceful.

The mountain is not on the Main Ridge but on the long lateral ridge running westwards to SRON NA CICHE.

The easiest ascent, although the most laborious, can be made by the STONE SHOOT. There is another easy way by a scree depression running up to the summit ridge between Sgumain and Alasdair. This south-west ridge gives a good scramble with its "mauvais pas" (very difficult); this can be avoided on the Ghrunnda side.

NORTH-WEST FACE

COLLIE'S CLIMB 800 feet DIFFICULT

This climb starts from the lowermost rocks. Probably the easiest way is up the Stone Shoot, then cross over right to the foot of the face.

The route goes straight up to the summit; it is easy to follow.

First ascent by J. N. Collie and party in 1896.

ABRAHAM'S CLIMB 800 feet DIFFICULT

Start from nearly the same place as Collie's but follow the left edge of a shallow gully running obliquely left; then an easy stretch towards the crest of the wall overlooking the Stone Shoot. Go straight up. The route is now easily followed.

First ascent by G. Abraham and party in 1907.

STONE SHOOT FACE

300 feet ap. VERY SEVERE at final chimney

Climb the first few pitches of Abraham's Route and where it overlooks the Stone Shoot take to this face and bear left and upwards. The rocks are not much more than difficult until a small amphitheatre is reached with overhangingly forbidding rocks all round. Climb up to the foot of the wall and from there follow a sloping ledge leading to a corner on the right, the holds on the wall are satisfactory (30 feet). Getting round the corner is very awkward as at the first glance there does not seem to be any handhold to get round but there is an undercut one for the right hand that supplies the key. The position now is an imposing one as the next move is up a greasy chimney with splayed out walls (basalt) overhanging the Stone Shoot. The chimney has to be forced by faith, friction and some jamming and has to be one continuous movement as the chimney is devoid of positive holds (boots). No belay for the traverse or the chimney could be found. The climb finishes up the North Arête.

First ascent by W. M. MacKenzie and A. M. Mac-Alpine in July 1937.

COIR' A' GHRUNNDA FACE

WEST GULLY   350 feet   DIFFICULT

This is the first definite gully one meets when traversing under the cliffs from the west and starts near a small grass patch. It is narrow and steep. There are eight short but hard pitches in quick succession for 200 feet, above which the open face is reached in a straight line below the summit.

First ascent by Steeple, Barlow and Doughty in 1912.

CENTRAL ROUTE   350 feet   VERY DIFFICULT

This route is right of the West Gully. The climb commences on a protruding buttress immediately to the left of a large cave. Follow the left edge of this buttress until a smooth vertical wall is encountered, traverse upwards left into a shallow gully. A few feet higher the climber is forced into a chimney on its left. This is the crux of the climb (90 feet). Above this the climbing is easier.

First ascent by Steeple and Barlow in 1921.

COMMANDO CRACK   250 feet   SEVERE

The climb starts below a crack running between two overhangings, about 100 yards left of the Thearlaich-Dubh Gap. It is about 30 yards left of a large black gully, which is a prominent feature of the face. There is also a prominent cave a few feet up on the immediate left.

Go up a rib, right of a crack for 10 feet and traverse into chimney on left, continuing up it to a pinnacle belay, high on left (40 feet). Climb wall on right a few feet and traverse into chimney. At overhang ascend with difficulty to block belay on left (60 feet). Return to crack on right and climb to sentry box below overhanging chockstone with belay (40 feet). Through route used. Get on to nose on left and up to stance and belay (40 feet). Layback ascent of right-hand crack, then cross to left crack; difficult ascent followed by 20 feet of scrambling (80 feet). Almost 100 feet of easier ground leads to right, ending at top of Alasdair Stone Shoot.

First ascent by A. C. Cain and B. L. Dodson in July 1950.

THEARLAICH-DUBH BUTTRESS
WEST FACE

300 feet   VERY DIFFICULT

Start under a small overhang near left-hand edge of buttress. Short traverse to right, follow a shallow groove until a corner leads on to a terrace. At left-hand edge of terrace is a steep slab topped by two overhangs. The slab is climbed by a crack and the first overhang is surmounted directly. From under the second overhang an awkward step is made to the left on to the very edge of the buttress which is followed to a stance and belay. Easier rocks until progress is barred by another series of overhangs. A traverse is made across the left wall of the buttress to a nose of rock projecting from the face. A steep shattered groove leads from the nose on to the summit of the buttress.

First ascent by K. Bryan and R. Jamieson on 18th July 1955.

SGURR SGUMAIN (3104 feet)

THE NORTH RIDGE   MODERATE

This well-defined ridge runs straight up to the summit from near the lochan.

First ascent by C. Pilkington and party in 1887.

FRANKLAND'S GULLY   400 feet   HARD SEVERE

This gully is really the left boundary of the North Buttress and is easily identifiable from the floor of the coire.

The start, cairned, lies up a steep slab, which is crossed from left to right to left, and at 20 feet a move round the edge leads to a triangular niche; beyond this is a steep 8-foot wall with no footholds, but a good handhold high up for the right hand enables a lodgement to be made on a slightly sloping mantleshelf. To attain a standing position is difficult, but once this is done an easy traverse leads into the bed of the gully.

Easy and moderate scrambling in bed of the gully leads to a cave belay (150 feet). Ascending traverse on true right wall to a recess, belay (20 feet). Traverse back to the bed of the gully on a rising ledge, which gradually gets narrower, and ceases before the bed of the gully is attained; the movement from the traverse to the gully is very difficult, belay (30 feet). A 70-foot crack, steep but not very difficult, ends abruptly on the north side of Sgumain; cairn.

First ascent by C. D. Frankland, M. M. Barker and H. V. Hughes on 4th August 1925.

NORTH BUTTRESS

This buttress faces west into upper Coire Lagan, and is cut off from the West Buttress by an easy gully. The wall of the buttress above the gully is undercut and teems with overhangs, and it appears very doubtful whether any route can be made up it. At the lowest point of the buttress the rocks are more amenable, while the quality of the rock at this point is the best on the buttress. This side of the buttress is conspicuous on account of two terraces which traverse across the face in an upward direction from left to right.

There are two routes on this buttress to date, one through usage has come to be known as Wood-Johnson's Route and the other is named the Direct Route. Height of the buttress is ap. 600 feet.

WOOD-JOHNSON'S ROUTE   HARD SEVERE

Starting at the lowest point of the buttress, just to the right of the gully (Frankland's Gully) separating the main crag from a pinnacle, the route goes up to a platform by way of a steep crack and the wall on its left (90 feet). The rock at this point is not very reliable, and all holds must be tested.

Frankland's Gully can be reached from this point. From the far side of the platform make an awkward stride into an open chimney, descend the chimney for 20 feet, and traverse into the gully.

The rocks above the platform overhang, and though it should be possible to climb directly upwards, the way taken is a traverse round the corner on the left, where an open chimney is climbed. The climbing is complicated by overhangs, which are difficult to overcome, since the holds, though good, are not usually obtainable until each movement has commenced. After 50 feet of climbing a stance and belay is reached by climbing an overhang on the left. The rock is very sound, and the holds when reached, are jughandles.

From the belay a partial hand traverse of 15 feet to

the right, followed by a short ascent, leads to the left-hand end of the lower terrace. The terrace is followed for about 150 feet until the foot of a steep crack is reached; this is climbed to the second terrace (40 feet), the finishing holds being excellent. Another traverse is made to the right, nearly to the edge of a gully. The rock above this terrace is exceedingly rotten, and great care should be taken in testing all holds. An ascent, directly upwards from a point a few feet short of the gully, leads to the top of the buttress.

First ascent by E. Wood-Johnson, C. J. A. Cooper and D. Levers.

DIRECT ROUTE   600 feet   VERY SEVERE

Climb first three pitches of Wood-Johnson's Route, branch up a wide, broken groove in the steep cliff to a rake sloping up to the right. After 80 feet of the rake climb prominent slab on the left. The last and hardest pitch follows. Climb an overhanging wall and move left to a steep slab ending on roof of buttress.

First ascent by D. D. Stewart, A. Colquhoun and P. V. Vaughan on 21st September 1951.

WESTERN BUTTRESS

There are now three climbs of considerable merit on this buttress—Superstition, Sunset Slab and West Trap Route, the last two starting from the traverse to the Sgumain Stone Shoot.

SUPERSTITION   350 feet   VERY DIFFICULT

The side of the buttress overlooking Coire Lagan has on it a prominent steep wall, about 150 feet high and about 200 feet up. The route starts directly under the left edge of the wall and about 150 feet below it, at the foot of a gully slanting left across the buttress.

Diagonal traverse to left up right-hand wall of gully to large sloping ledge (80 feet). Up easy slabs to right to grassy terrace. Up wall and over slabs to foot of chimney, left corner of prominent wall (70 feet). Climb slabs to immediate left of chimney to belay (40 feet). Traverse into chimney and go up to a large ledge and belay (30 feet). Move right along sloping ledge and up steep corner. Traverse left across steep slab and up corner to finish (50 feet).

First ascent by J. D. Foster, J. R. Stead and B. L. Blake on 13th July 1951.

SUNSET SLAB   500 feet   HARD SEVERE

From Coire Lagan the prominent white blaze at foot of long steep crack. This is reached by about 100 feet of scrambling. Above, the crack is blocked by an overhang and appears impossible. The route uses steep slab slanting left from the crack. The only sound belay is 30 feet below the foot of the slab.

Up slab to stance and belay in crack below small overhang (90 feet). Up overhang and up slab and a corner crack until one reaches a steep crack on right bounding wall of slab (110 feet). Up crack (45 feet). Easy traverse right to foot of deep-cut crack (140 feet). Up steep strenuous crack (90 feet). Continue up crack to effect junction with West Trap Route (100 feet)—and up 150 feet of latter.

First ascent by J. D. Foster and B. L. Blake on 13th July 1951.

WEST TRAP ROUTE   800 feet   SEVERE

The central part of the climb follows the line of a con-

spicuous trap dyke, to the left of which is a much shorter
dyke, and still more to the left the conspicuous white
blaze. Starting from the traverse the initial problem is
to climb up to the trap dyke above the lower overhang.
Thereafter the line of the dyke is followed to the upper
shattered west ridge. The climb can be completed by
Steeple and Barlow's route on the final tower.

The climb starts up a little chimney. Shortly after is
a small mantleshelf problem, then a traverse to right and
ascent to beneath the main difficulty. The pitch is 30-40
feet and is balance and pull (less difficult than Crack of
Doom). Above this a traverse to left brings one to a
crack between a detached mass of rock and the main
mass. Above, one ascends 40 feet or so and traverses to
left on to the dyke. The rest of the climb is along this.

First ascent by J. H. B. Bell and F. S. Smythe in
July 1924.

FINAL TOWER DIRECT   SEVERE

The route from the north-west corner works upwards
across the north face, treading back to the right near the
top.

First ascent by Steeple and Barlow in 1920.

The lower part of the buttress is crossed by an easy
rake—the continuation apparently of the Cioch "Terrace". By taking this rake anyone going from Coire
Lagan to the Sgumain Stone Shoot will save a long
descent.

LADIES' PINNACLE, situated on the Sgumain Stone
Shoot gives a short climb. First climbed by Mrs Phillip
and Miss Prothero.

SRON NA CICHE
COIRE LAGAN FACE

The precipice of Sron na Ciche, facing north-west-wards, is about a mile in length, and nearly 1000 feet high in the middle.

A moderately difficult well-defined rake, the "Ter-race", crosses the face at a steep angle, sloping upwards from east to west. It leaves the Sgumain Stone Shoot near the foot of the rocks, leads into the Eastern Gully above the lowest pitch, passes right round the Cioch Slab to the Cioch Gully, which it crosses at an arch formed by a huge jammed block, and after a short hiatus runs up to the top of the precipice near the summit of the West Buttress, passing under the "Flake" —where there is a second short break—and the "Finger".

EASTERN BUTTRESS

ZIG-ZAG ROUTE   MODERATE

The route commences at a rake high up on the Stone Shoot, crossing the buttress to the upper part of the Eastern Gully.

First ascent by Professor Collie in 1907.

MAGIC CASEMENT   315 feet   VERY SEVERE

Immediately above the point where the Terrace meets the Sgumain Boulder Shoot some prominent boulders abut against a bulge in Eastern Buttress. Above this there is a slabby bay (start of the Girdle Traverse). Above this again is a small squat buttress cleft by a crack in its centre. This is the start of the climb. It lies perhaps 70 feet lower than the start of Zig-Zag Route.

Up to the crack by large blocks and into it. Belay and cairn on scree ledge above (40 feet). Take the right-hand of two open grooves. Layback and delicate slab above lead to a belay position astride an edge. Back left by a stomach-traverse under leaning flakes, then upwards by easier rocks to ledges and belays on the lower, scree-covered rake of Zig-Zag Route (30 feet). Walk across, and slightly up this rake *circa* 30 feet to climb the upper-most crack leading to the Upper Rake of Zig-Zag Route. Up the crack. At the top walk up 10 feet of the easy ground of the Upper Rake to the foot of an imposing vertical crack, the crux of the climb (25 feet). The crack is climbed past a bollard-spike to an inserted chockstone. From the chockstone the pitch is artificial (35 feet). Up the groove to its back, through a cracked overhang, and up a steep groove above to a ledge with a cairn (25 feet). Climb a left-slanting groove directly behind the cairn, and return up right to a ledge. Continue to another ledge with good belays (30 feet). Climb a steep crack just right of a basalt dyke and cross it to finish left up a glacis (60 feet). Scramble to the summit of the buttress.

First ascent by Maynard M. Miller and G. H. Francis on 21st June 1953.

CARAVAN ROUTE   270 feet   MILD SEVERE

An outward bulging corner 30 feet right along the flat ledge at the top of the first pitch of the Girdle Traverse. Start here.

Up the corner and the wall above with a trend to the right until at 80 feet it is possible to leave the slab bounded on its right by a wall, cross the wall at a break. Stance and belay after a few feet. Here the climb touches on the Direct Route (95 feet). The blocks above and slightly to the left of the stance lead to a corner and beyond (20 feet). Slightly left again and up, to a steep wall with slanting cracks up its centre. Take the cracks to a belay at the top (70 feet). The easier slabs on the right lead to the Direct Route below its penultimate pitch (80 feet).

First ascent by G. W. S. Pigott and A. S. Pigott on 9th June 1949.

DIRECT ROUTE   600 feet   VERY DIFFICULT

Starting from the Terrace and running up the front of the buttress. The edge of the buttress, overlooking the Eastern Gully, is adhered to as much as possible. The route is now well marked.

First ascent by Steeple, Barlow and Doughty in 1912.

CHIMNEY ROUTE   DIFFICULT

Starting at the same level and a short distance west of the Direct Route. It follows a well-marked series of chimneys and right-angled corners running up the steep wall of Eastern Gully. There are eight pitches, the fourth a fine 60-foot chimney.

First ascent by Steeple and Barlow in 1912.

EAST WALL ROUTE   900 feet   SEVERE

Start at very foot of buttress, just left of Eastern Gully (as for Hangover).

Easily diagonally up left followed by left traverse to a scooped slab, climb with difficulty, again left and up across slab on small holds. Go left and across an open corner then up and across slabs to a good ledge. Easily up a gully and then left to Terrace. Cross Terrace then diagonally up and across smooth slab to overhung ledge; awkward left traverse to small stance. A difficult left traverse below overhang (near scree), then up edge of groove left by decaying basalt dyke. Climb the dyke and over slab used by Girdle Traverse. Go left and up obvious fault going round the corner out of the amphitheatre, then steeply up a crack to an airy perch. Strenuous movement up and left on apparently insecure blocks. Orient Wall above on left. First pitch of wall, just below large thin flake traverse up right to steep crack in wall on left of large rough easily angled slab, then by crack on right to good stance and belay. Round left to large split blocks. Traverse right upwards to a good ledge. High step to shelf on right. Now level with top of final wall of Direct.

First ascent by R. E. Davies and C. B. Machin in August 1947.

HANGOVER ROUTE   170/200 feet   VERY SEVERE

Route starts 30 feet to left Eastern Gully from a corner. From a good ledge and belay at 50 feet an overhanging corner is surmounted, then a slab on the right leads to a mantleshelf recess on left. An overhanging corner gives way to a catwalk crack running obliquely up and left-wards. From top of this the climber moves gradually towards Eastern Gully and finishes there.

First ascent by D. H. Haworth and J. G. Ritchie on 17th May 1947.

EASTERN GULLY   VERY SEVERE

The difficulties lie in the first two pitches, the second in particular being very severe. This can be avoided by starting at a point about 50 feet below the cave, an 8-foot wall on the left is climbed by a steep crack to a pinnacle.

The rest of the gully is easy. There is a fork further up, either branch can be climbed.

First ascent by Steeple and Barlow in 1913. The second pitch by Haggas and Thompson in July 1938.

THE CIOCH

The first climber to explore the Sron na Ciche cliffs was Professor Collie and attracted by this rather remarkable pinnacle, now known as the Cioch, he made its earliest ascents in 1906. His route goes up the deep crack, now well scored, on the left side of the Great Slab and overlooking the Eastern Gully, which is entered above the second pitch and ascended for a short distance until an easy ledge, the "Shelf", leads down to the narrow neck behind the Cioch. There are other routes on the Great Slab, nowhere more than difficult and well scored by countless pairs of nailed boots. The Cioch can also be climbed by a fine airy route from the west side up the right-angled corner, perhaps difficult.

CIOCH BUTTRESS

PETRONELLA   180 feet   SEVERE

A small buttress lies between Eastern and Little Gullies. Start from the screes up a prominent crack which curves leftward up the centre of the buttress. The crack is awkward. The overhangs above are turned by a shelf on the left and an airy pull-out.

First ascent by G. H. Francis and E. A. Wrangham on 29th June 1952.

LITTLE GULLY   DIFFICULT

This is the small gully to the west of Eastern Gully. Without difficulty follow either of the parallel branches until they converge below a fine cave pitch, which is climbed by backing up and out through a window above the entrance.

The next pitch goes direct but can be turned on left.

Above this the gully becomes a shallow groove, which

G

is left, and a traverse is made on the face to the left. A few feet of diagonal ascent lead to the lower terrace.

First ascent by G. Barlow.

BASTINADO   375 feet   VERY SEVERE

Starts 60 feet to the left of Cioch Grooves (cairn). Ascend to obvious crack sloping slightly left, climb this to broad grassy ledge (120 feet). Directly up corner for 25 feet then up to the left to sloping ledge. Belay for thin line only (35 feet). Traverse 6 feet left below groove which overhangs at its lower end. Climb with difficulty (a sling can be useful here) until good holds allow a move to be made right to a triangular corner (piton belay) (40 feet). Climb crack immediately behind corner and follow it for 120 feet to small rock ledge (120 feet). Continue up crack to large ledge below the Cioch.

First ascent by J. Cunningham, J. Allen and W. Smith on 16th July 1956.

CIOCH GROOVES   475 feet   VERY SEVERE

Start on wide, easy ledge leading from screes to second pitch of Cioch Direct. Keep to the left of this all the way to the Terrace, though it is very close to the older route at the latter's first crux (Chimney). First and third pitches are long and exacting. On both a piton is used. Close to "Chimney" of Cioch Direct a horizontal left traverse gives access to easier grooves leading to the Terrace.

First ascent by I. G. McN. Davis and G. H. Francis on 21st September 1951.

CIOCH DIRECT   400 feet   MILD SEVERE

This well-known climb follows a chimney which starts from the screes a few feet below a large cairn. The features above the chimney are a steep nose, traverse left under some blocks, above this a traverse right, some steep climbing and then two parallel cracks.

First ascent by H. Harland and Ashley Abraham in 1907.

CIOCH WEST   400 feet   VERY DIFFICULT

50 feet to the right of the Direct Route up a difficult chimney. 100 feet of easier rocks to an awkward slab. Above this a horizontal ledge to the right to a flake. Steep climbing to a small ledge, a short chimney and then the left traverse, after that easier rocks. A well-marked climb.

First ascent by C. F. Holland, H. R. C. Carr and Miss D. E. Pilley in 1919.

CIOCH GULLY   SEVERE

The start can be made either by a water course or by dyke lines on either side. Higher up there are two hard pitches.

First ascent by Buckle and Barlow in 1906.

UPPER CIOCH BUTTRESS

LEFT EDGE ROUTE   250 feet   MILD SEVERE

The start of the route is in the innermost corner of the deep recess on the ledge between the Cioch and the Eastern Gully. The recess is well seen from Coire Lagan on the left-hand edge of the Upper Cioch Buttress, it bounds the Great Slab on the upper left and continues to the summit of the buttress.

The first 60 feet is in the recess then an upward traverse

to the right on to the edge of the buttress. Climb straight
up the edge and the route ends where the glacis coming
up from the Crack of Doom runs on to the summit
plateau.

First ascent by W. M. MacKenzie and A. M. Mac-
Alpine in July 1937.

INTEGRITY   250 feet   SEVERE

Start at a cairn on the Shelf, a few feet above the
grassy platform behind the Cioch. Climb recess, emerging with difficulty on to the steep slab above. Make
straight for the sloping glacis above Crack of Doom.
Turn an overhang on the right and surmount another
direct. Later the fault widens and contains large
jammed blocks.

First ascent by D. A. Haworth and I. a'p. E. Hughes
on 11th July 1949.

WALLWORK'S ROUTE   250 feet   DIFFICULT

Starting from the col behind the Cioch the route goes
straight up the buttress.

First ascent by W. Wallwork, H. M. Kelly and J.
Wilding in 1915.

ARCHER THOMSON'S ROUTE
              250 feet   DIFFICULT

Starting from the col behind the Cioch the route
traverses the upper cliff, obliquely to the right. 50 feet
along a protruding corner; afterwards mount a recessed
corner to a big platform. The rest is easily followed.

First ascent by J. M. Archer Thomson and party in
1911.

RIB OF DOOM   250 feet   VERY SEVERE

This rib is on the left of the Crack of Doom.

The lowest section is very steep and smooth but it can be avoided by first groove of Crack of Doom. Then one gains the edge of the rib by a subsidiary groove. Follow the rib to the top (very exposed).

First ascent by C. M. G. Smith and A. Cleland, June 1949.

CRACK OF DOOM   250 feet   SEVERE

The crack may be reached from below by ascending the 100-foot gully of the Girdle Traverse, or alternatively, by the section of the Traverse which leads from the knife-edge behind the Cioch to the Terrace.

The final 20 feet are the hardest.

First ascent by D. R. Pye and L. G. Shadbolt in August 1918.

DIRECT FINISH TO THE CRACK OF DOOM
SEVERE

Immediately above the Crack of Doom this route goes straight up very steep rocks.

First ascent by A. S. Pigott and J. Wilding in 1921.

DIRECT APPROACH TO CRACK OF DOOM
200 feet   SEVERE

This affords a convenient and pleasant approach route to the Crack of Doom from the Cioch area. Start about 30 feet higher up the Cioch Gully than the grass terrace leading right from the gully below the Hexagon Block; and a few feet below large chockstone in the gully.

A square corner is ascended for 6 feet to a short slab giving on to a line of holds leading diagonally right to an open V. Left side of V ascended to a small stance

and belay on a detached block (70 feet). Return to foot
of V and go upwards to the right round another slab—
up a steep corner to a narrow ledge (60 feet). Traverse
right from the ledge for 8 feet and ascend a steep shallow
groove which then joins the lower section of the Crack
of Doom about 50 feet below the Terrace.

First ascent (probably) by Brenda Ritchie and C. D.
Milner in June 1936.

CRACK OF DOUBLE DOOM
300 feet   HARD SEVERE

This lies on the wall between Crack of Doom and
Central Gully Arête, starting on the steep slab just right
of Crack of Doom and finishing above right-hand apex
of this slab by ending in a right-angled crack. It is severe,
hard of its kind in rubbers and is probably harder than
its prototype. Half-way up an awkward move circum-
vents a flake at the top of the recess near the apex of
the slab.

First ascent by D. H. Haworth and I. a'p. E. Hughes
on 21st May 1947.

DOOM FLAKE   300 feet   SEVERE in rubbers

Start 25-30 yards up the Terrace from Crack of Doom,
to the right of a large cube of fallen rock, where there is
a larger fallen flake of rock forming a right-angled corner
with the main face. Starting cairn is at the left side of
flake below a thin crack in the wall above. A basalt
jig-saw is encountered a short distance below the large
flake, situated half-way up the crack.

First ascent by D. H. Haworth and I. a'p. E. Hughes
on 21st May 1947.

CENTRAL GULLY DIFFICULT

An interesting climb, fairly straightforward. Above the point where the Amphitheatre is reached and after several steep pitches there is an unclimbed one which can be turned on the left wall. After this the gully forks, the left one is more interesting.

First ascent by A. G. Woodhead, E. W. Steeple and H. E. Bowron in 1907.

EAST WALL AND ARÊTE OF CENTRAL GULLY
(above Amphitheatre) DIFFICULT

From above the Amphitheatre the east wall of the Central Gully can be followed to the Terrace; then an interesting arête on the edge of the gully leads to the summit.

First ascent by Barlow, Buckle and Doughty in 1909.

WESTERN BUTTRESS
THE AMPHITHEATRE WALL
600 feet VERY SEVERE

The start is in the Amphitheatre, to the west of and slightly lower than the Hexagon Block. About 300 feet up, the Terrace crosses it at a slant. Above this is the upper wall, up which the route goes from about 20 feet to the right of the Flake. The lower wall is in three sections, (a) slabs and walls, (b) a crack and (c) steep imposing wall.

The slabs are steep and holdless. The first runout leads to a belay (55 feet). Traverse 25 feet to the right (belay) straight up for 25 feet, severe, to a terrace. Two embryo chimneys, belay (35 feet). A V.D. slanting crack (25 feet) followed by a crack with three jammed blocks, exposed, stance. Bridging pitch, stance, and belay (25 feet). The crack continues at an easier angle to a spike belay (75 feet). The Terrace is 20 feet above.

From a cairn 20 feet to the right of the Flake by left and right to a large corner (30 feet). A huge poised block marks this point. 20-foot traverse to the right, spike belay and stance. Above and to the right is an overhang, and then a 20-foot groove, stance and belay. Upwards for 10 feet, obliquely upwards to right for 15 feet, across a steep rake to belay and stance. Up pinnacle on right, then 5 feet up to a leftward hand traverse, belay. Upwards to left over jammed blocks and on to the plateau (60 feet). A formidable climb of continuous severity.

First ascent by A. Horne and H. V. Hughes on 22nd July 1932.

AMPHITHEATRE ARÊTE   DIFFICULT

Starting from above the introductory section of the Cioch Gully, climb up slabs to the Central Gully where it reaches the Amphitheatre then turn off right across water-worn slabs until the nose of arête leading to point 2507 is reached; follow this to the top.

First ascent by Professor Collie in 1907.

MALLORY'S SLAB AND GROOVE
900/1000 feet   SEVERE

The commencement is to the left of the Central Gully, up a crack immediately to the right of a large overhang. From a stance at the top a slab is climbed for 8 feet and a difficult stride is then made to the right. An exposed traverse is then made across smooth slabs to the Central Gully. Climb the gully for 60 feet then a crack on the right for a further 60 feet to a large block. Ten feet higher an awkward traverse is made to a perch. The lower part of the crack on the left is climbed, with a turning movement on the slabs to the right to the

groove above the crack. Great care is required owing
to the long run-out. Above the groove a difficult corner
is ascended, and a 20-foot crack leads to a sloping shelf.
A traverse to the right and a steep ascent of 50 feet leads
under an overhang to a difficult corner, from which a
crack is followed for 40 feet up to the right, when the
arête of the West Central Route is joined. The gully on
the left of the arête is then ascended.

First ascent by G. H. L. Mallory, D. R. Pye and L. G.
Shadbolt in 1918.

DIAMOND SLAB   600 feet   VERY SEVERE

Start at small overhang 15 yards right of Malloy's
Cairn.

Climb overhang, a right traverse and crack to slab
below overhang. Belay in crack (100 feet). Left traverse
and crack to grass platform to boulder belay in Central
Gully (90 feet). Cross gully on to steep slab climbed
direct on large sloping holds, trend left to knob belay in
shallow corner (120 feet). Traverse up right, then
straight up to grassy ledge with two small flake belays
(70 feet). Traverse up right on good ledge broken by
sloping slabs, small flake belay (100 feet). Continue
traverse to vertical trap line, this followed to West
Central Gully.

First ascent by A. Allsopp and R. G. Marsley on
19th July 1946.

TRAP FACE ROUTE   1000 feet   VERY SEVERE

Climb the Central Gully or, better still, the first two
pitches of Slab and Groove, and round a corner to the
right in Central Gully from the continuation of Slab and
Groove is a well-marked chimney below the line of the
West Central Arête. Follow the chimney for about 60

feet, then trend rightwards and up below a small nose of rock to a corner. From here a line of very steep and awkward cracks leads up through the line of steep rocks above. Follow the trap depression which goes up to the right of overhangs, passing a bridged boulder, to the rake of Zig-Zag Route. The trap continues above this for a short distance, then loses itself in a small amphitheatre of trap rock. From here there are several lines to the summit of the buttress. (1) Follow the easy groove leading up to the right then up a severe crack trending slightly leftwards then more easily rightwards and on to a ridge just below and to the right of the summit ridge of the buttress. (2) Climb directly up a short way then follow a diagonal fault up and left to a huge detached flake with a fine crack separating it from the buttress, then up the crest of the West Central Arête, or just to the right of it.

First ascent by J. B. Burrell and C. N. Cross in 1914.

This is a very fine route and less artificial than Slab and Groove; it has a better continuous standard. The cracks are inclined to be greasy and not too pleasant in wet conditions.

TRAP FACE ROUTE (variation)
150 feet   VERY SEVERE

From stance after rounding the corner from Mallory's Route ascend about 10 feet up the layback crack in corner. Ascend right wall of corner, working diagonally right to overhanging, undercut ledge at the right of a shallow chimney. Climb this and move right to shallow groove, ascended with difficulty until one moves back left into the corner. Climb this to a stance and belay.

First ascent by A. C. Cain and B. L. Dodson in July 1950.

Perhaps this is a more fitting section than the original one.

ANGEL'S PAVEMENT   330 feet   SEVERE

The climb starts from Central Gully at a point about 200 feet above the screes (an arrow is scratched on the rocks).

Over steep rocks trending leftwards towards the top. Poor belay and no stance (170 feet). Up and bearing slightly to the right over steep rocks (80 feet). An ascending righthand traverse which leads to the prominent V when viewed from Central Gully (80 feet).

First ascent by M. North, M. Grundy and J. Roberts on 13th July 1955.

CENTRAL SLABS   300 feet   SEVERE

This route commences at a grassy patch in Central Gully, just above the point where the gully becomes almost horizontal, and lies over steep slabs to the finish directly above in West Central Gully.

The first pitch is 150 feet of steep slabs; ending at a narrow, sloping grass ledge with belay; a ledge lower down can be used to bring up the third man (if one) on 100 feet of rope.

The next section is over an overhang by a steep crack, the holds in which need careful testing. A belay is reached a few feet above the overhang on the left (50 feet).

The final pitch lies up slabs at an easier angle, and finishes in West Central Gully, just under the crack in the upper overhangs. From here a variety of routes may be followed.

First ascent by E. Wood-Johnson, C. J. A. Cooper and D. Levers.

CENTRAL ROUTE   850 feet   HARD SEVERE

The climb starts on a steep wall just left of the point where Mallory's Route leaves the Central Gully. (Cairn).

Mallory's Route can be used to the point where it leaves Central Gully, so giving a total climb of about 1000 feet.

In all there are 12 pitches from the Central Gully to where the climb finishes up a steep tower to the highest point of Sron na Ciche. This fine climb is a succession of walls, cracks, slabs and overhangs. The route bears up leftward for two pitches then right upwards to the two prominent cracks on Mallory's Route (beneath the big slab). Straight up for 50 feet. The route now bears slightly left towards the Amphitheatre Arête and keeps on a parallel with it until it merges with the Arête in its upper part; leave the Arête and descend to the right into shallow gully beneath final tower. The tower probably gives the hardest bit of climbing on the whole route.

First ascent by D. Leaver and J. Gott in July 1951.

WEST CENTRAL GULLY AND ARÊTE CLIMB
1000 feet   VERY DIFFICULT

Climb this gully or rake to where it terminates near the overhang which is a marked feature on this face. Turn the overhang on the left, cross to the right of the arête, past a large block seen from the screes. Bear somewhat left but keep to the general line of the arête.

First ascent by Barlow and Buckle in 1908.

ZIG-ZAG CLIMB   DIFFICULT

Climb West Central Gully for about 300 feet, leave it for a line of trap dyke and climb this for 100 feet. Two chimneys to a grassy platform, then follow two ledges, first to the left, the second to the right. A grassy chimney leads to the arête of West Central Route.

First ascent by Shadbolt, McLaren and E. S. Reynolds in 1911.

CHIMNEY AND CRACK CLIMB   Severe

Leave the West Central Gully about 250 feet above the screes, and ascend slabs on the right to a long vertical cave which is climbed by the left wall. Above the cave mount the rocks straight up to a deeply-cut chimney (bridging). Follow to the left a steep sloping ledge for a few yards, and then back to the right, past a steep corner to a platform. Now follow a long crack (110 feet) finishing over a bulge (severe).

First ascent by J. M. A. Thomson, H. O. Jones and Miss B. C. Jones in 1911.

ENGINEER'S SLANT   1000 feet   Very Difficult

This is an interesting climb as it takes the climber from the foot of the West Central Gully across the face of the Western Buttress to the Amphitheatre Arête near the summit.

The route can be traced out on the West Buttress Diagram. Start from the foot of the West Central Gully, branch to the right where that gully becomes a crack, go between Crack and Chimney Variation and Median Route, take in part of the Zig-Zag Route and by a final grassy chimney to the West Central Arête. Straight ahead, at the other side of the wide shallow gully between this and the Amphitheatre Arête, the route continues, another chimney leading out on top of the crag. The first part of this climb is the better.

First ascent by D. L. Reid, Sale and Brown in June 1932.

MEDIAN ROUTE   1000 feet   DIFFICULT

This route goes more or less up the centre of the Western Buttress.

Start 45 yards west of the Central Gully, mount a long crack to a grass slope and cross the West Central Rake, above which an oblique chimney is followed to the right to a mass of overhanging rocks. These rocks are cut by two chimneys; the left one is approached by an exposed slab. Then a short traverse to the right, and an ascent of a fan-like formation of overhanging rocks. Finally a shallow chimney and easy rocks.

First ascent by Steeple and Bowron in 1911.

A. B. ROUTE   850 feet   SEVERE

This route starts halfway between the foot of the Central Gully and the foot of West Central Route.

300 feet of easy slabs are climbed, then a traverse of 60 feet left on a grassy ledge, followed by 200 feet of steep slabs and then an exposed traverse of 100 feet left across a trap dyke to a grass ledge. 250 feet of very steep and exposed slabs on good holds are climbed to the point where West Central Route and Trap Face Route meet. The finish can be made up Trap Face Route, giving a climb of approximately 1100 feet.

First ascent by A. Armitage and Miss H. Broadbent in August 1936.

BOOMERANG   700 feet   HARD VERY DIFFICULT

Start (cairn) in an enclosed chimney 30 yards east of West Central Gully and work up and left over slabs and a water-worn slab corner into West Central Gully just below the point where the Median crosses it. Now the line is up to the right, easily across Engineer's Slant, into a conspicuous trap fault below a light-coloured wall.

The fault, twice awkward, still runs up and right to a grassy finish.

First ascent by D. D. Stewart and D. N. Mill on 11th September 1952.

CORONATION   500 feet   SEVERE

Just below a short pitch in the grassy introduction tongue of West Central Gully and 60 feet left of Parallel Cracks. Start is an overhung recess in the upper wall. Climb the recess by the right then trend left to a lay-back crack. A long groove now leads more easily upwards to a patch of thick grass. Climb an undercut bulge then a short leftward trend. The formidable wall above this is turned by a fine crack on the left, easier than it looks. The next overhang is climbed by a difficult movement on the wall on the left, the crux of the climb. One short easier crack remains.

First ascent by D. D. Stewart and party *circa* July 1953.

PARALLEL CRACKS ROUTE
500 feet   VERY DIFFICULT

This climb commences at the foot of the rake of the West Central Route, on a steep rib bounding a large slabby depression. Of two parallel cracks, that on the right is joined about halfway up the climb, with a turning movement on the edge of the depression. The left-hand crack is gained at a height of 150 feet and steep slabs climbed to a platform. Some short pitches and a stiff crack lead to a fine 40-foot chimney containing an arched block. Easier ground is followed to the edge of Western Gully.

First ascent by Steeple, Barlow and Doughty in 1920.

COOPER'S GANGWAY   800 feet   VERY SEVERE

This climb has previously been referred to as the Western Buttress.

The climb is in the area which is bounded by the West Central Route and the Western Gully. The route commences at the foot of steep slab about 50 feet to the right of the foot of West Central Gully and just to the right of two small overhangs. The slab is climbed until the climber is forced to its left edge, a stance and belay being reached a little higher (90 feet). From here slightly right fairly easy climbing in 140 feet to a large grass platform, above and between two grass patches. A short upward traverse to left leads to a ledge at foot of steep wall. To the left, and after 50 feet to a wide dyke, above the dyke is another slab. Cross the dyke, traverse slab to left and over low wall, belay. Position exposed on overhanging wall overlooking the foot of West Central Route. Rocks above appear rotten but short steep crack climbed, no difficulty. Easy rocks lead to steep wall (light coloured rock). Take steep sloping gangway, which appears to lead to a good stance on the left edge of the wall (very severe). Easy rocks to the top of buttress.

First ascent by C. J. A. Cooper, E. Wood-Johnson and D. Levers.

APEX ROUTE   800 feet   SEVERE

On the buttress between West Central Route and Western Gully. As seen from the coire, the route lies directly up the centre of the narrow-pointed buttress, crossing Parallel Cracks en route and appears to keep to the right of Cooper's Gangway.

Start at a crack at the lowest point of the slabs forming the base of the buttress (cairn). After about 200 feet cross a rake and climb above this, always trending left, crossing a number of slabs and over several steep ribs. A number of difficult pitches are encountered, including a vertical chimney, a crack in an overhanging wall, a strenuous slanting chimney and two steep narrow slabs flanked on the right by vertical walls. The route finishes at the apex of the buttress.

First ascent by J. Wilkinson, D. W. Jackson and H. Ironfield (through leads) in July 1946.

WESTERN GULLY   MODERATE

The gully starts 200 feet above the screes and contains numerous pitches nowhere difficult.

THE GIRDLE TRAVERSE   VERY DIFFICULT

Leave the Sgumain Stone Shoot at a large hollow (cairn), above the easy terrace leading to the Eastern Gully and traverse round the Eastern Buttress to the foot of the "60-foot chimney" on the Chimney Route. After ascending a slanting ledge on the gully wall for about 100 feet, and descending a narrow 40-foot chimney containing Serpentine Rock, some narrow ledges and a delicate hand traverse lead to the chockstone of the second pitch of the gully. Cross the Cioch Slab to the neck behind the Cioch and follow a ledge under the Upper Buttress. Traverse a little pinnacle and some slabs and descend an oblique chimney to the Terrace. Follow this for 20 feet to the west and descend a shallow gully for 100 feet, then a movement left to the sloping mossy roof of the Hexagon Block.

Cross the Central Gully to the Amphitheatre (lowest point reached), and traverse water-worn slabs to above the nose of the Amphitheatre Arête (cairn on sky-line). The West Central Arête is then crossed and an ascending

H

line taken, passing above the "Crack" of the Chimney and Crack Route. Eventually a point is reached beyond the Western Gully about the same level as the starting point. Allow $5\frac{1}{2}$-6 hours for a competent party of two as this route gives about 2000 feet of rock climbing.

Recorded by Steeple and Barlow in 1912.

GIRDLE TRAVERSE (Variation)   SEVERE

From the Amphitheatre the traverse is continued below Collie's cairn and continued across Slab and Groove to West Central Route. Median Route is crossed and finish made 100 feet above the finish of Parallel Cracks Route. Severe in rubbers and more in keeping with the first part of the climb.

THE FLAKE AND FINGER

The "Flake" stands on the Terrace and overlooks the wall of the Central Gully.

The "Finger", a pinnacle a little further west along the Terrace, is about 60 feet high on the outside.

GHRUNNDA FACE
LOWER CRAGS OF COIR' A' GHRUNNDA

These crags lie on the south-east side of the ridge of Sron na Ciche, facing Sgurr nan Eag across the lower corrie. A watercourse divides the line of rock into two sections, which have been named the South and North Crags. The South Crag is steep and slabby, and gives the best climbing. A rake—the Pinnacle Rake—runs diagonally upward from right to left across the upper part. The North Crag is more broken, and is divided by a large gully into two portions, of which that on the left has been called the Stack Buttress, and the right-hand portion the Slab Buttress. There is also a northerly extension, but the rocks here are small and indefinite.

SOUTH CRAG

THE FAR SOUTH BUTTRESS
500 feet   MODERATE

On the left of the Green Recess Chimneys. Slabby rocks are ascended for about 250 feet to the foot of a tower which is climbed by its left edge to the Pinnacle Rake. Above this a harder pitch leads to a second tower, which is also climbed on the left.

First ascent by Steeple and Barlow *circa* 1920.

GREEN RECESS CHIMNEYS
600 feet   DIFFICULT

These chimneys form the first continuous break at the south end of the crag. The climb commences on a stony rake. A number of interesting pitches lead to a semi-circular green recess below the Pinnacle Rake. Above the Rake a second series of pitches gives a fine finish to the climb.

First ascent by Steeple and Barlow *circa* 1920.

CENTRAL BUTTRESS   700 feet   DIFFICULT

From the stony rake a rock ledge—the Horizontal Ledge—runs across the central part of the face at a height of about 130 feet above the scree. The remarkably steep and smooth rocks below the Ledge are climbed by means of a narrow curving dyke-line. The buttress is then attacked on the left side of a projecting rib. The centre of the buttress is followed as nearly as possible with a traverse to the left edge below the Pinnacle Rake. The tower above the Rake gives fine climbing to its termination on the summit ridge.

First ascent by Steeple and Barlow *circa* 1920.

TRAP DYKE ROUTE   MODERATE

A long trap dyke immediately to the right of the
Central Buttress gives an interesting but not difficult
climb. Where the route crosses the Pinnacle Rake it
passes a lofty pinnacle, one of two from which the rake
is named.

WHITE SLAB ROUTE (Ordinary Route)
600 feet   DIFFICULT

The climb starts to the left of a large rock depression
120 feet high and near the South Crag Gully. Cross the
roof of the depression and from the far side the rock wall
is ascended to a chimney, the right of two, climb this for
40 feet then move to a rib on the right. From there a
platform is reached below the White Slab. Steep rocks
are climbed to a ledge with a large block, and a traverse
made to the left across the head of a chimney to a recess.
Ascend a rib of rock to the Pinnacle Rake. Above this a
rock wall and a fine 40-foot chimney lead to the open
buttress, thence to the summit.

First ascent by Steeple and Barlow *circa* 1920.

WHITE SLAB DIRECT   600 feet ap.   SEVERE

Start up the large rock depression to the right of the
ordinary route.

Climb slabby rocks to a stance and belay. Follow a
crack in a V-shaped groove for 15 feet, and step out to
the right on to a platform (no definite belay). Cross the
groove and climb a slab on its left side by three thin
ledges. Traverse left and climb straight up to the top of
the large depression, where the ordinary route is joined
on the Horizontal Ledge.

Continue directly up the "crack on the left side of the roof". Then follow easier rocks straight to the foot of the White Slab.

Starting from the bottom corner of the slab an upward traverse on tiny holds leads to the outer edge of the slab. From here 8 feet of easier rock is followed to the roof of the slab. Complete the climb by the same finish, above the Pinnacle Rake, as that of the ordinary route.

First ascent by G. H. Francis and J. M. Brown on 14th April 1950.

WHITE SLAB, OXFORD VARIATION
180 feet   VERY SEVERE

Start at the foot of the little buttress between the Rock Depression and the South Crag Gully. Climb up 40 feet to a ledge at the foot of a small scoop to a stance and belay. Continue up scoop, then left and right to gain the foot of a slab (lower edge overhangs). It is cleft by two cracks—take the right hand one; it is wet and overhangs (piton as running belay). Keep the line of the crack for 70 feet to a small platform. Step up 5 feet on to the outer and lower part of the Horizontal Ledge.

First ascent by G. H. Francis, R. H. Holhouse and P. F. Nutson on 28th August 1950.

SOUTH CRAG GULLY   400-500 feet   DIFFICULT

Shallow trenches on the right are climbed for 200 feet, then a short mossy pitch, a chockstone pitch and a difficult chimney. A cave pitch, a leaf of rock and several small pitches lead to the Pinnacle Rake, above which the gully dwindles to a crack; climb the rocks to the right.

First ascent by Steeple and Barlow *circa* 1920.

GIRDLE TRAVERSE OF SOUTH CRAG
600 feet.   VERY DIFFICULT (HARD)

Start from left end of the crag at a cairn on a large mossy ledge and traverse into Green Recess Chimneys at about the foot of the first chimney proper and keep as near as possible to a level of about 40 feet below the foot of White Slab. The first hard pitch is directly below the Slab, a delicate traverse along a thin crack to the foot of a grassy groove (40 feet), then 30 feet upwards to the large grassy ledge at the foot of White Slab Tower. The second hard pitch is from the right-hand edge of the large ledge up a broken perpendicular corner for 20 feet then a very delicate traverse across the gully to belay (50 feet).

First ascent by V. J. Wiggin and E. Wood-Johnson in May 1947.

THE OWL BUTTRESS LEFT
180 feet   MODERATE

This climb starts to the right of South Crag Gully and works gradually rightward up a series of slabs. From a horizontal shelf a V-shaped chimney leads to the rake to the left of Owl Pinnacle. Rocks above easy but interesting.

First ascent by E. W. Steeple and G. Barlow in July 1924.

THE OWL BUTTRESS RIGHT
180 feet   SEVERE

Start left of Owl Chimney, left of the extremely steep rocks. First pitch diagonally right to belay above steep initial section. Slabs above slightly right avoid easier ground on left. Final pitch steep little wall, ending at top of Owl Pinnacle (very rotten). Rubbers or vibrams.

First ascent by D. Levers, C. J. A. Cooper and E. Wood-Johnson.

OWL CHIMNEY   150 feet   DIFFICULT

At the extreme right of the crag, the lower part is constricted, the middle V-shaped, and the upper part overhangs, but is easily climbed on the right.

First ascent by Steeple and Barlow *circa* 1920.

NORTH CRAG

THE STACK BUTTRESS (Direct Route)
500/600 feet.   DIFFICULT

Climb the right-hand edge of the buttress overlooking the dividing gully as directly as possible to a rake below the Stack. Ascend a steep but rough slab and the face of the Stack by a narrow vertical crack. The rocks above are easy.

First ascent by Steeple and Barlow *circa* 1920.

THE STACK BUTTRESS (Red Wall Variant)
DIFFICULT

A little to the left of the Direct. A wall of red trap, a broken rib of gabbro, and a long chimney to the rake beneath the Stack.

First ascent by Steeple and Barlow *circa* 1920.

NORTH CRAG GULLY AND BLACK KNIGHT'S WALL   500/600 feet   DIFFICULT

The lower part of the gully is turned by the rocks of the Slab Buttress. The upper part widens out, with an overhanging cave pitch on the right. The centre of the wall is climbed, passing a large upright block—the Black Knight.

First ascent by Steeple and Barlow *circa* 1920.

THE SLAB BUTTRESS   800 feet   MODERATE

The buttress is in three sections divided by rakes. Start at its lowest point. Rock rough and clean.

First ascent by Steeple and Barlow *circa* 1920.

THE PEAKS OF SGURR DUBH

Sgurr Dubh is a long lateral ridge running eastwards with three separate and well-defined summits, Sgurr Dubh na Da Bheinn (3069 feet) on the Main Ridge, Sgurr Dubh Mor (3089 feet) and Sgurr Dubh Beag (2420 feet). The ridge is easy except for a steep pitch on the west face of Sgurr Dubh Beag; this can be avoided by traversing from the col round the south side.

From Loch Coruisk the long eastern ridge gives an easy climb on ice-ground rocks.

Two past presidents of the Club once paid a visit to Sgurr Dubh, and their doings were duly chronicled by the Club poet.

> Said Maylard to Solly one day in Glen Brittle,
> "All serious climbing, I vote is a bore;
> Just for once, I Dubh Beag you'll agree to do little,
> And, as less we can't do, let's go straight to Dubh Mor."

> So now when they seek but a day's relaxation,
> With no thought in the world but of viewing the views,
> And regarding the mountains in mute adoration,
> They call it not "climbing" but "doing the Dubhs".

There is a moral behind the insertion of these lines.

CAISTEAL A' GHARBH-CHOIRE

The Caisteal is on the main ridge on the north side and close to the bealach of the same name.

Good sport can be had here; the rock is perhaps the roughest in the Cuillin—painfully adhesive it is said.

Climbs are short. The traverse is moderate and the North End Direct is difficult; ascended by W. W. Naismith and party in 1912.

SGURR NAN EAG (3037 feet)

THE CHASM   400 feet   VERY DIFFICULT

A prominent block S-shaped cleft in the steep mass of rock on the Garbh-choire side of south-east ridge, about midway between the summit and the bealach. There are four pitches, the final one the hardest where combined tactics may be necessary. An interesting gully.

First ascent by Steeple, Barlow and Doughty in 1919.

WESTERN BUTTRESS   600 feet   HARD DIFFICULT

The buttress is split into three indistinct ridges, the route is on the left-hand and most prominent of these.

Start at the foot of the steep lower section; a line of short cracks and chimneys is followed up the centre of the ridge. From the final steep section 100 feet of climbing to a broad terrace. A short traverse to the right leads to a steep little groove by means of which the right-hand corner of the ridge is climbed. A few minutes' walk leads to the northern summit of Sgurr nan Eag.

First ascent by R. S. Dodson, B. W. Smith and H. Booth in May 1948.

COIRE NAN LAOGH GULLIES

The three prominent gullies at the head of Coire nan Laogh are named West, Central and East Gullies.

WEST GULLY is easy.

CENTRAL GULLY   DIFFICULT

First a square chockstone, climb on left. Then an

undercut pitch, climb by slab on left, traverse back to
left. Above this a long trap chimney leads to a pitch
with bridged boulders.

EAST GULLY is moderately difficult.

First ascents by Herford and Laycock in 1912.

SGURR A' CHOIRE BHIG (2880 feet)

On the north side of this peak is a small crag; this can
be reached by a descending rake from the bealach between the peak and Sgurr nan Eag. There are two
gullies—the East and the West—of moderate difficulty;
and also the North-East Ridge is long and well-defined
but no more than of moderately difficult standard.

First ascents by Steeple, Barlow and Doughty in 1921.

GARS-BHEINN (2934 feet)

This is regarded as the true termination of the Cuillin
Ridge. The ascent is repaying as a view-point. Its
North-East Ridge is an interesting route for anyone
going to or from Loch Scavaig.

MARSCO (2414 feet)

WEST-SOUTH-WEST CRAG

ODELL'S ROUTE   500-600 feet   DIFFICULT

Part of this crag is seen in profile from Sligachan.

From near the centre of amphitheatre, slabs and
grooves for *circa* 250 feet to scree patch. Make for the
shoulder above prominent central buttress (380 feet).
Climb steep rock above shoulder (cairn) *circa* 200 feet.

Rock of excellent quality (coarse dusty granophyre)
and the whole crag seems to be worthy of further
exploration.

N. E. Odell, 19th July 1943.

CENTRAL BUTTRESS (WRANGHAM'S ROUTE)
550 feet   DIFFICULT

A route up this buttress forming right-hand edge of the amphitheatre. There are steep smooth walls with corners on the left.

Start at foot of rocks. Ascend fairly directly by the corners till the top wall is reached. Go round to the right of this up to the shoulder. Here Odell's route is joined.

First ascent by E. A. Wrangham on 22nd August 1953.

THE BLAVEN GROUP

The group can be reached from Sligachan in several ways:

(1) Follow the Glen Sligachan path nearly as far as the march fence, then turn off to the left and ascend the glen round the back of Marsco. Then go along the top of or across the south-west slope of Garbh-bheinn to the north end of the Clach Glas ridge.

(2) Follow the Glen Sligachan path as far as Loch an Athain, and strike up Coire Dubh to the north end of the Clach Glas ridge.

(3) As in (2) but go past the loch and climb Blaven first.

(4) Past the head of Loch Slapin to the foot of Blaven's east slopes.

BELIG is out of the way and does not afford much climbing.

GARBH-BHEINN has a steep face to north-east on which some rock-climbing can be had.

SGURR NAN EACH is a rocky ridge, half a mile long running eastwards from the col between Garbh-bheinn and Clach Glas. This ridge is much broken and gives easy, but interesting, scrambling. The north face has a considerable extent of broken indefinite rock.

The most prominent ridge was climbed by H. Raeburn in September 1898.

CLACH GLAS (2590 feet)

Clach Glas is the great rock tower on the ridge connecting Garbh-bheinn with Blaven. The ridge is well broken up and gives quite a delightful climb. The first ascent of Clach Glas was made in 1888 by a shallow gully in the west face running up to the south of the summit—Charles Pilkington and party.

WEST FACE

NAISMITH'S ROUTE   MODERATELY DIFFICULT

Start about midway between the lowest rocks and the shallow gully of the original ascent. Bear left towards the Black Cleft (not yet climbed). The summit ridge is gained north of the top.

First ascent by W. W. Naismith and J. A. Parker in 1896.

CONSOLATION GULLY   MODERATE

To the left of Black Cleft. Three-pitch climb.

First ascent by A. P. Abraham and party in 1907.

ARCH GULLY   MODERATE

Below the Garbh-bheinn and Clach Glas Bealach; a big chockstone pitch half-way up, two or three pitches and a natural arch higher up.

First ascent by A. P. Abraham and party in 1907.

EAST FACE

The East Face is of steep broken rock mixed with grass ledges and may be traversed in many places. The main features on this side are the two gullies A and B, which run up the face starting at a height of 1000 feet and finishing on the summit ridge on each side of the highest point. On the face near the top of Gully B are several detached pinnacles, climbed in 1896 by Naismith and Parker.

A long rake runs obliquely left up the middle of this face.

CENTRAL BUTTRESS   DIFFICULT

This buttress lies between the two gullies and it is likely no two parties will follow the same route on the lower section. The ascent is by ledges connected by steep walls until the angle becomes too severe when a ledge leads to the foot of a chimney 60 feet high near the South or "A" Gully. Above this the rocks are more broken and the summit is reached south of the top.

First ascent by W. N. Ling and E. Backhouse in June 1915.

"B" GULLY   VERY DIFFICULT

The first eight pitches are good, one pitch high up is quite hard. Above this the gully is easy and the fine buttress on the right can be gained by a subsidiary grass gully and followed to a prominent tower which can be passed on the left and the summit reached by an indefinite route up slabs.

First ascent by G. D. Abraham, H. Harland and G. Summers in June 1920.

SOUTH-EAST ROUTE   DIFFICULT

There is a prominent tower on the Blaven-Clach Glas
Bealach, the lower rocks of which extend well down the
eastern screes. Between these rocks and Clach Glas is a
deeply-cut gully with a very steep north wall. The
climb is on this north wall, starting just below where the
gully emerges on to the screes. The start is just to the
left of a deep black chimney and leads up past some
bright green patches of grass. The route now lies by
face and chimney to the broken ground some 200 feet
below and to the south of the summit cairn. About
three-quarters of the way up the climb is crossed by a
transverse slab (moderate).

First ascent by J. C. Thomson and J. R. Young in
June 1914.

TRAVERSE OF CLACH GLAS RIDGE
MODERATE

Clach Glas is usually crossed by following the main
ridge from end to end in either direction. In going
from north to south the first part presents no great
difficulties, and any obstacles there are can be easily
turned—usually on the right. On reaching the foot of
the final tower a conspicuous slanting gully will be seen,
which starts a little west of the col, and by this gully the
steep roof of the tower is gained without trouble. The
summit rocks can also be climbed straight up from this
col. (Difficult.)

The descent of Clach Glas southwards towards Blaven
is easier than it looks if one remembers to keep to the
left. Start down a crack on a sloping slab for 30 feet,
followed by a rather rotten and narrow arête 60 feet in
height.

From the Clach Glas-Blaven Bealach a descent on
either side can be easily made by scree slopes, but

climbers descending to Coire Dubh should make sure that they have reached the real col before beginning the descent. At the Bealach is a small grassy hollow that might almost do for a "putting green".

BLAVEN (3042 feet)

Blaven is now usually climbed from the Clach Glas Bealach, the traverse of the two mountains giving a fine expedition.

When the weather is misty the route is rather hard to follow and the following directions may perhaps be of use:

From the Bealach avoid a steep pitch on the left; climb an easy 12-foot wall, then cross scree to the right; pass one chimney and mount the second (a stone shoot), which leads to a scree platform, at the upper (eastern) end of which stands Naismith's "HALF-CROWN PINNACLE" (climbed 1893), the top of which is close to the Blaven upper screes. Go along this scree platform to the left a few yards, then climb a 60-foot chimney, which gives a climb up its right-hand wall. From the top of it cross some big stones, and go down into a large stone shoot, climbing up which to the left leads to a cairn on the sky-line above the Blaven precipices, at a height of 2600 feet. This "large stone shoot" may be used in the descent of Blaven, but it leads down into Coire Dubh a long way below the col.

Two other routes to the Blaven screes from the saddle behind the "Half-Crown Pinnacle" are:

(1) Is very short, but not easy, especially if the rocks are wet. It starts from a point a few yards down the Sligachan side of the saddle. The Blaven rocks rise steeply for 12 or 15 feet, but they can be climbed to a narrow ledge which slopes upwards to the left and leads to the upper screes.

(2) By crossing the saddle behind the Pinnacle, and going down the easy gully on its east side for a few yards, a place will be found where it is quite easy to climb the Blaven wall, and get on to the "roof".

Blaven can be ascended by the tourist along its delightfully easy south ridge from Camasunary. This is little more than a pleasant walk; the view from the top is very fine.

The western slopes of Blaven may be descended for 1000 feet by the scree gully between the two tops (Mr Willink's route). Further down, the gully steepens and seems to be impossible, but a short distance above the difficulty the climber can escape from the gully to the buttress on either side. Both these buttresses offer easy but interesting routes when ascending Blaven from the west.

The summit can also be reached from the north-west by way of the scree shoot from Coire Dubh, already referred to, and this route is the quickest way down when making for Sligachan.

From Broadford the usual route is to mount the scree slopes from Coire Uaigneich to the north top, or Mr Willink's original route by the great gully which separates the two tops may be followed.

NORTHERN OR PINNACLE RIDGE   MODERATE

This is a prominent feature of the north face of Blaven, as seen from Loch an Aithain. After 300 feet the ridge is indefinite but higher up it again narrows.

First ascent by Dr Clark, T. E. Goodeve and Harry Walker in April 1905.

SOUTH-EAST BUTTRESS   MODERATE

This is the buttress on the north side of the great scree-filled gully which separates the two tops of Blaven. The route, which is rather indefinite, lies over easy slabby rocks and up trap dykes.

First ascent by H. MacRobert, R. A. Brown and W. A. Morrison in 1907.

EAST RIDGE   MODERATE

This is the spur which runs east from the north top of Blaven. The only difficulties are the ascent of the lowest pinnacle and in the passage from it to the second. There is a fault, 2 feet wide, which runs straight to the top of the lowest pinnacle.

First ascent by Sidney Williams and party (no date).

C. D. BUTTRESS   MODERATE

The buttress between gullies C and D. The route lies up the centre over glacier-worn rocks to a protruding belt of rock. Keep left up cracks and steep grass and a narrow deep chimney. Above this the route crosses the left fork of D gully to the right and joins Williams' route at the second pinnacle.

First ascent by J. C. Thomson and J. R. Young in June 1914.

SGURR NA STRI

WEST FACE

Routes can be made straight from the water's edge to the summit giving excellent sport and over 1600 feet of climbing on slabs, cracks and ledges.

Reported by M. B. Nettleton on 28th April 1934.

The view from Sgurr na Stri is very fine, including the Western Cuillin, has a bird's eye view of Coruisk, Blaven and Clach Glas.

I

No. 1. THE BLACK CUILLIN

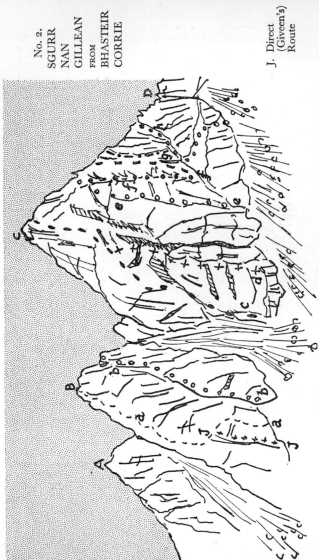

No. 2.
SGURR
NAN
GILLEAN
FROM
BHASTEIR
CORRIE

A. Third Pinnacle
B. Knight's Peak

a. West Face—Ordinary Route
b. Subsidiary Gully

e. Flutings Climb
f. Deep Chimney

J. Direct
(Given's)
Route

No. 3. NORTH FACE OF AM BASTEIR AND
         THE BHASTEIR TOOTH

A to B.   Chimney Route, Am Basteir
A to C.   Traverse across North Face
D to E.   King's Cave Route
D to F.   North Chimney

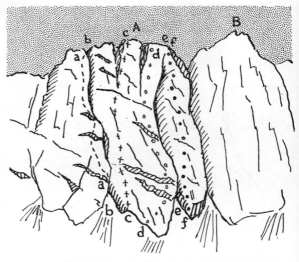

No. 4. AN CAISTEAL FROM HARTA CORRIE

A.	An Caisteal	c.	Raeburn's Route
B.	Sgurr na Bhairnich	d.	Thomson's Route
a.	South Buttress Route	e.	North Gully
b.	South Gully	f.	North Buttress Route

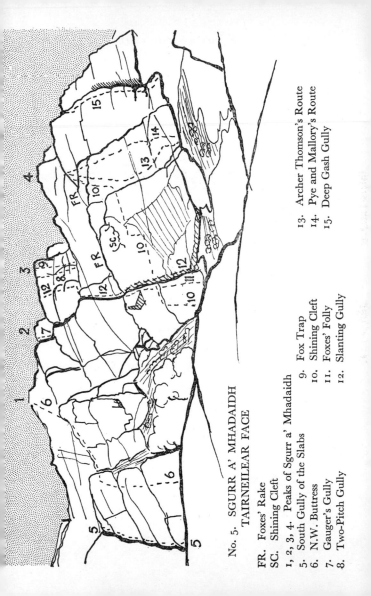

No. 5. SGURR A' MHADAIDH
TAIRNEILEAR FACE

FR. Foxes' Rake
SC. Shining Cleft

1, 2, 3, 4. Peaks of Sgurr a' Mhadaidh
5. South Gully of the Slabs
6. N.W. Buttress
7. Gauger's Gully
8. Two-Pitch Gully

9. Fox Trap
10. Shining Cleft
11. Foxes' Folly
12. Slanting Gully

13. Archer Thomson's Route
14. Pye and Mallory's Route
15. Deep Gash Gully

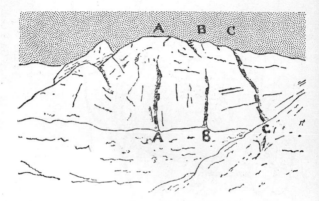

No. 6. WEST FACE OF SGURR A' GHREADAIDH

A. Hidden Gully B. Vanishing Gully C. Diagonal Gully

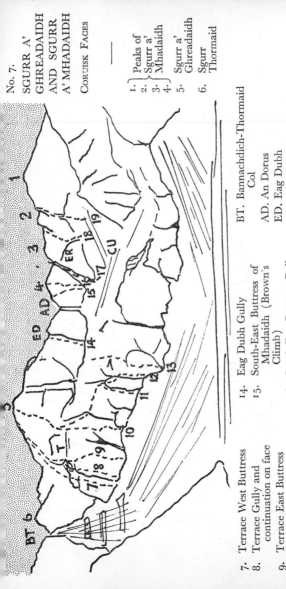

No. 7.

SGURR A'
GHREADAIDH
AND SGURR
A' MHADAIDH

CORUISK FACES

——————

1. ⎫ Peaks of
2. ⎬ Sgurr a'
3. ⎭ Mhadaidh
4. ⎫ Sgurr a'
5. ⎬ Ghreadaidh
6. Sgurr Thormaid

BT. Bannachdich-Thormaid Col
AD. An Dorus
ED. Eag Dubh
T. The Terrace
CU. Coire an Uaigneis
ER. Easy Rake in Mhadaidh

7. Terrace West Buttress
8. Terrace Gully and continuation on face
9. Terrace East Buttress
10. South-East Ridge Direct
11. Collie's Route
12. Slab Route
13. Coruisk Buttress (approx. line)

14. Eag Dubh Gully
15. South-East Buttress of Mhadaidh (Brown's Climb)
16. South-East Buttress Gully
17. 3-4 Gully
18. 2-3 Gully
19. 1-2 Gully

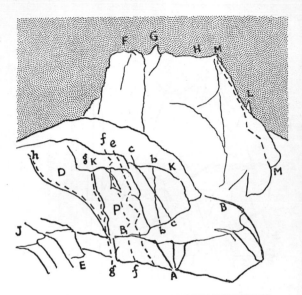

No. 8. THE CLIFFS OF BEALACH BUTTRESS.

A.   The Arrowhead.
BB.   The Terrace (Bealach
         Buttress).
D.   The "unclimbable"
         wall.
E.   Screes below Rotten
         Gully.
F.   An Stac.
G.   Inaccessible Pinnacle.
H.   Summit of Sgurr Dearg
J.   The Terrace (Sgurr
         MhicCoinnich).
KK.   The Upper Terrace.
L.   Rock Tower (Sgurr Dearg), M. O'Brien and Julian's
         Climb (Sgurr Dearg).

*a*A. Line of approach from
         Bealach Coire Lagan
*A*bb. Lost Arrow.
*A*cc. The Bow.
*A*dd. Hourglass Crack.
ee.   Gemini.
ff.   Pinnacle Face.
P.   The Pinnacle.
gg.   Black Cleft.
gh.   Thunderbolt Shelf

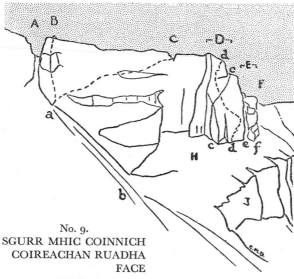

No. 9.

SGURR MHIC COINNICH
COIREACHAN RUADHA
FACE

A. Bealach Mhic Coinnich
B. Sgurr Mhic Coinnich, summit cairn
C. Top of "Easy Rake"
D. The Fluted Buttress of Sgurr Mhic-Coinnich
E. The N.E. Buttress of Sgurr Mhic-Coinnich
F. The 2595-foot Col, and head of "Rotten Gully"
H. The Terrace, Sgurr Mhic Coinnich
J. The lower cliffs of Sgurr Mhic Coinnich, unclimbed
a-B. Forgotten Groove
a-C. Easy Rake
A-b. Approach to the Terrace from the south
c-c. Crack of Dawn
d-d. Fluted Buttress Route
e. N.E. Gully, O'Brien and Julian's
f. Start of N.E. Buttress Route
F-f. Approach to the Terrace from the north, via "Rotten
       Gully"

The diagram is based on photographs taken from Sgurr
Coire an Lochain

No. 10.

MHIC-COINNICH,
THEARLAICH, ALASDAIR
AND SGUMAIN FROM
SGURR DEARG

A. Sgurr Mhic Coinnich
B. Bealach Mhic Coinnich
C. Sgurr Thearlaich
D. Head of Alasdair Stone Shoot
E. Sgurr Alasdair
F. Sgurr Sgumain

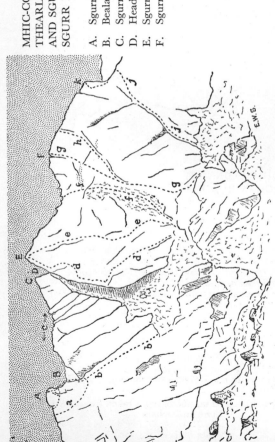

a. Easy route to summit of
    Sgurr Mhic Coinnich.
    Upper route near Sum-
    mit is Collie's Ledge.
b. West Buttress Route, Sgurr
    Mhic Coinnich

c. Gullies of Sgurr Thearlaich
    A, B, C, D, E, in order
    from left to right
d. Abraham's Climb
e. Collie's Climb

g. Northern Buttress, Sgurr
    Sgumain
h,j. Easy routes to Sgurr
    Sgumain
k. Terminal Tower direct,
    North-Western Buttress

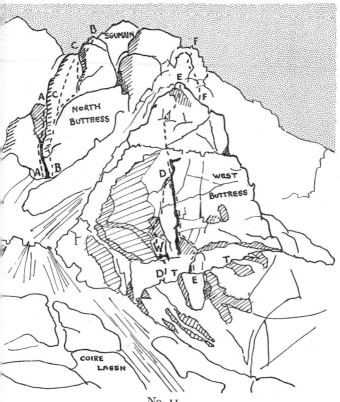

No. 11.

NORTH AND WEST BUTTRESSES OF SGUMAIN

A-A.	Frankland's Gully
B-B.	Wood-Johnson's Route
C-C.	Direct Route
D-D.	Sunset Slab
E-E.	West Trap Route
F-F.	Final Tower Direct
T-T-T.	Easy Rake to Sgumain Stone Shoot
W.	White Blaze

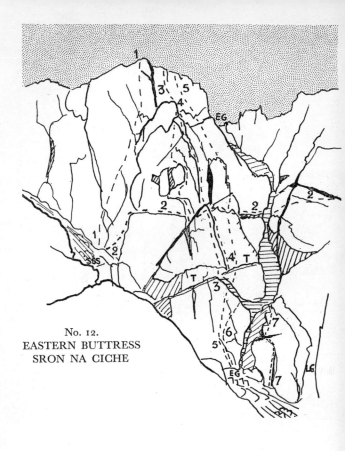

No. 12.
EASTERN BUTTRESS
SRON NA CICHE

SSS. Sgumain Stone Shoot	2. Girdle Traverse
T. Terrace	3. Direct Route
EG. Eastern Gully	4. Chimney Route
LG. Little Gully	5. East Wall (approx. line)
1. Magic Casement (approx. line)	6. Hangover Route
	7. Petronella

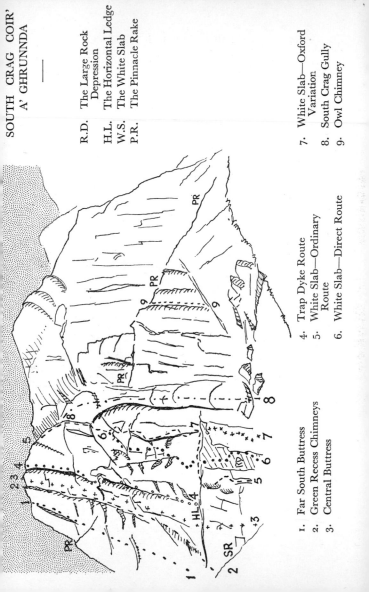

SOUTH CRAG COIR' A' GHRUNNDA

R.D. The Large Rock Depression
H.L. The Horizontal Ledge
W.S. The White Slab
P.R. The Pinnacle Rake

1. Far South Buttress
2. Green Recess Chimneys
3. Central Buttress
4. Trap Dyke Route
5. White Slab—Ordinary Route
6. White Slab—Direct Route
7. White Slab—Oxford Variation
8. South Crag Gully
9. Owl Chimney

No. 14.   UPPER CIOCH BUTTRESS, SRON NA CICHE

For details of routes see facing page

K

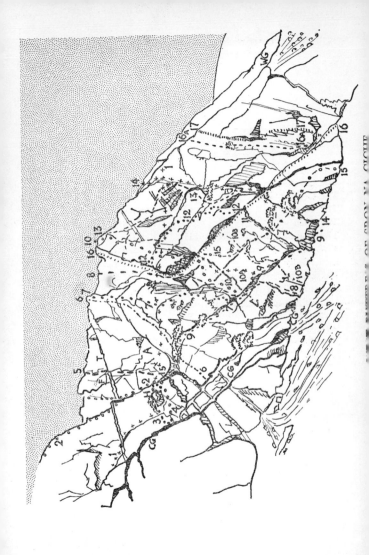

SKETCH MAP OF GROVE N. GÖTHE

A. Amphitheatre
F. Flake
T. Terrace
H. Hexagon Block
CG. Cioch Gully
WG. Western Gully
1. Girdle Traverse
2. Central Gully Arête
3. Route over Hex. Block
4. Route under Hex. Block

5. Amphitheatre Wall
6. Amphitheatre Arête
7. Central Route
8. Mallory's Slab & Groove
9. Central Gully
10. Trap Face Route
10A. Angel's Pavement
10B. Diamond Slab
11. Central Slabs
12. Zig-Zag Route

13. Crack and Chimney Route
14. Median Route
15. A.B. Route (approx. line)
16. West Central Gully and Arête
16A. Coronation (approx. line)
17. Parallel Cracks Route

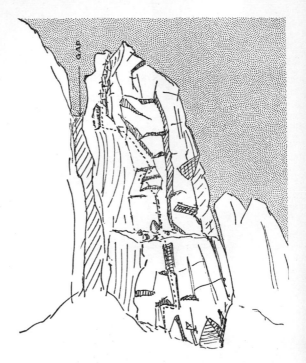

No. 16.   THEARLAICH DUBH BUTTRESS

No. 17.   CLACH GLAS—WEST FACE

A to B.   Arch Gully
C to D.   Consolation Gully
E to F.   Black Cleft (unclimbed).
G to H.   Naismith and Parker's Route.
J to K.   Pilkington's Route

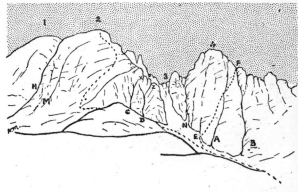

No. 18. BLAVEN AND CLACH GLAS
EAST FACES

1. Blaven, S. top.   3. Clach Glas Bealach
2. Blaven, N. top   4. Clach Glas

The dotted lines show the easiest route to Blaven and an easy
scramble up Clach Glas.

H. Great Gully (Original Route)
M. S.E. Buttress
C. and D. Gullies
N. Gully between Bealach Tower Buttress and Clach Glas
A. and B. Gullies

INDEX TO ROUTES AND ROCK CLIMBS

CLASSIFICATION OF CUILLIN CLIMBS

THE Standard British System of Easy, Moderate, Difficult, Severe and Very Severe has been kept. Moderately difficult has been introduced, and the Severes split into three categories: mild, ordinary and hard.

LEGEND		LEGEND	
E	Easy	MS	Mild Severe
M	Moderate	S	Severe (ordinary)
MD	Moderately difficult	HS	Hard Severe
VD	Very difficult	VS	Very Severe